Understanding rituals

Rituals are at the core of the social identity of all communities. Yet each society varies in its view of what is ritual and what is not. *Understanding Rituals* explores how ritual can be understood within the framework of contemporary social anthropology, and shows that ritual is now one of the most fertile fields of anthropological research.

The contributors look at ritual as a special kind of performance, which is both an act and a statement. They discuss the views of Frazer, Van Gennep, Robertson Smith and Marcel Mauss, and explore the different aspects of ritual activity in order to question the validity of current theories. They also analyse specific rituals taken from a wide range of societies: they link Vedic times to the present situation in India, a Christianized Moluccan society to its still current pre-Christian social structure and values, contrast the different modes of participation in a Nuba village in Sudan, and describe the confrontation between Punjabi and English communities in a London suburb.

Understanding Rituals shows how rituals create and maintain – or transform – a society's cultural identity and social relations. By examining these rituals, both in particular and in general, the contributors enable us to discover the ultimate and contradictory values to which each society as a whole is attached. The book will therefore be of great value to all students and teachers of social anthropology and cultural studies.

Daniel de Coppet is Directeur d'Etudes at the Ecole des Hautes Etudes en Sciences Sociales in Paris.

EUROPEAN ASSOCIATION OF SOCIAL ANTHROPOLOGISTS

The European Association of Social Anthropologists (EASA) was inaugurated in January 1989, in response to a widely felt need for a professional association which would represent social anthropologists in Europe and foster co-operation and interchange in teaching and research. As Europe transforms itself in the nineties, the EASA is dedicated to the renewal of the distinctive European tradition in social anthropology.

Other titles in the series

Conceptualizing Society
Adam Kuper

Revitalizing European Rituals
Jeremy Boissevain

Other Histories
Kirsten Hastrup

Alcohol, Gender and Culture
Dimitra Gefou-Madianou

Understanding rituals

Edited by
Daniel de Coppet

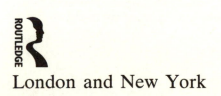
London and New York

First published in 1992
by Routledge
11 New Fetter Lane, London EC4P 4EE

Simultaneously published in the USA and Canada
by Routledge
a divison of Routledge, Chapman and Hall Inc.
29 West 35th Street, New York, NY 10001

© 1992 Daniel de Coppet

Phototypeset in Times by Intype, London
Printed and bound in Great Britain by
Biddles Ltd, Guildford and King's Lynn

British Library Cataloguing in Publication Data

A catalogue record for this book is available from the British Library.

Library of Congress Cataloging in Publication Data

Understanding rituals / edited by Daniel de Coppet.
    p.   cm. – (European Association of Social Anthropologists)
    Includes bibliographical references and index.
    1. Rites and ceremonies.   2. Ritual.   I. Coppet, Daniel de.
    II. Series: European Association of Social Anthropologists (Series)
    GN473.U47   1993
    390–dc20   92–5657
                                                                      CIP

ISBN 0–415–06120–2
      0–415–06121–0 (pbk)

Contents

Contributors

Gerd Baumann is Lecturer in Social Anthropology and Senior Tutor at Brunel University. He was awarded a Ph.D in 1980 from Belfast University. He has conducted fieldwork in the Nuba Mountains of Sudan and in South Asian communities living in London.

Michel Cartry is Directeur d'Etudes at the Ecole Pratique des Hautes Etudes (section des sciences religieuses), where his teaching concerns African religions. He has been director of the URA (Unité associée de recherche) at the Centre National de la Recherche Scientifique: Systèmes de pensée d'Afrique Noire. He has conducted fieldwork among the Gurmantche in Burkina-Faso.

Daniel de Coppet is Directeur d'Etudes, Ecole des Hautes Etudes en Sciences Sociales, Paris. He has engaged in long-term fieldwork in the Solomon Islands, making six expeditions since his first in 1963, and he has also done fieldwork in the Moluccas. His publications include many articles and (with H. Zemp), *'Are 'Are: Un peuple Mélanésien et sa musique* (Paris: Editions du Seuil, 1978).

Raymond Jamous is a Research Fellow in Social Anthropology at the Centre National de la Recherche Scientifique. He holds a Doctorate in Social Anthropology (1977) from Paris V Université René Descartes and has conducted fieldwork in Berber communities of the Rif in Morroco and among the Meo community in India.

Charles Malamoud, Agrégé de l'Université, Docteur ès-lettres, has been the student of both Pr. Emile Benveniste and Pr. Louis Renou. He has taught Sanskrit at the Universities of Lyon and Strasbourg. From 1972 to 1977 he was Maître-assistant at the Ecole Pratique des Hautes Etudes and in 1977 became Directeur d'Etudes at the Ecole Pratique des Hautes Etudes (section des sciences religieuses).

David Parkin has been Professor of African Anthropology at the School of Oriental and Asian Studies, University of London, since 1981. He was awarded a Ph.D in 1965 and has conducted extensive fieldwork in different societies of Eastern Africa. He is Chairman of the Association of Social Anthropologists of Britain and the Commonwealth.

J. D. M. Platenkamp is Lecturer in Cultural Anthropology at the Department of Cultural Anthropology and Sociology of Non-Western Societies of Leiden University, The Netherlands. He holds a Doctorate in Social Sciences (1988) from Leiden University and has conducted fieldwork in North Halmahera and South-East Seram (Indonesia), on which he has reported in several publications.

Introduction

Daniel de Coppet

This volume contains the six contributions prepared for the panel 'Understanding Ritual', which met at Coimbra on September 2, 1990, in the framework of the first conference of the European Association of Social Anthropologists. 'Understanding Ritual' was one of four related panels, the other three being 'Constructing Genders', 'Making History', and 'Conceptualizing Societies'. These four themes were and are an invitation to discuss the fund of anthropological knowledge in the light of current world trends. That this discussion unfolds in a European framework implies a double comparison: intra-European, of course, but also between anthropological ways of thought in Europe and in the rest of the world, particularly in the United States.

Our discussion takes place at a moment when social anthropology, which since its creation has contributed, together with sociology, to the elaboration of contemporary ideologies, is joining with other disciplines, including philosophy, in a vast questioning of social science discourse. The social dimension of what is human is currently the object of far-reaching debate, given the planet-wide standardization of certain cultural traits and the astonishing contrast between this standardization and the vitality of specific cultures, with their faculty for integrating contradictory influences without, for all that, losing their sense of identity. At this first conference of the EASA, it seemed interesting to open a discussion not only on general themes such as history in anthropology, the social construction of gender differences, and the scientific understanding of societies but also on a domain of social life often considered puzzling, that of rituals.

Indeed, while rituals are discerned and described by most

anthropologists as matters of the greatest interest, they remain a topic of lively discussion which from the beginning has divided the scientific community and which has often touched on the very essence of the subject. Successive scholars assign new characteristics to rituals, sometimes contradicting those previously suggested, with the result that they begin to appear an inexhaustible, mysterious constellation in the firmament of the social sciences – a curious domain discerned by all of us but glimpsed differently by each of us. Could it be that we anthropologists unanimously agree on the visibility of ritual only because we all adhere to the same modern ideology, shaped in the West, for which the opposition between ritual and non-ritual is founded as much upon the Book as upon so-called reality? This question leads to a second of more general import: Does anthropological perception recognize in every collective identity a kind of distinction between ritual and non-ritual, albeit assuming different forms in different societies? If this is so, we will have identified one of the bases of the social dimension and the necessary and sufficient condition for the comparison of societies – that is, for the practice of anthropology itself.

Let us accept for the moment that this distinction – ritual/non-ritual, symbolic/real, religious/secular, ceremonial/everyday – constitutes the social dimension par excellence, composed of tension and/or harmony but composed always of this distinction and this inseparability. And let us recognize that Durkheim, in his quaintly ardent language – that of the origins of our discipline – seems to have had this intuition when at the conclusion of his *Elementary Forms of Religious Life* he wrote,

> a society can neither create nor recreate itself without at the same time creating ideal(s). This creation is not a sort of work of supererogation for it, by which it would complete itself, being already formed; it is the act by which it is periodically made and remade. Therefore when some oppose the ideal society to the real society, like two antagonists which would lead us in opposite directions, they materialize and oppose *abstractions*. The ideal society is not outside of the real society; it is part of it. Although we are divided between them as between two poles which mutually repel each other, we cannot hold to one without holding to the other; for a society is not made up merely of the mass of individuals who compose it,

the ground which they occupy, the things which they use, and the movements which they perform but above all is the idea which it forms of itself.

(Durkheim 1925 [1912]: 603–4, my emphasis)[1]

In conjunction with this early sociological intuition we must also acknowledge Dumont's effort to call attention to the hierarchical dimension of social life and to shed light on the fundamental social fact that 'situations [are] to be distinguished by value' (1980:244), opposing the modern tendency to let '*facts*' be considered independently of *values*' (p. 244). The distinction between ritual and non-ritual is a constituent of the hierarchy of values which shapes our Western society's social relations.

Durkheim's intuition may, however, be accepted only if one immediately adds that the inseparability of ritual and non-ritual cannot be founded on the variation from one society to another of ritual alone, with the non-ritual term remaining identical for all societies, a sort of universal 'real' confronted equally by all of them. To do so would simply elevate our Western conception of what is 'real' to the status of a universal standard. On the contrary, there is reason to believe that, if societies are in fact constructed around this difference between ritual and non-ritual, the non-ritual varies as well from one society to another and constitutes a different object for each.

If the definition of the indissoluble pair 'ritual/non-ritual' is specific to a particular collective identity, then we have in this relation of each society to its own object a sort of universal, one which permits the obvious though only incipient mutual understanding of cultures. To glimpse such a universal is simultaneously to reject the relativism that is in good measure responsible for the enormous dangers confronting the contemporary world. It fully corroborates our fieldwork experience, validating it as 'natural' as well as necessary, and illustrating it may constitute a programme capable of uniting the scientific community and, simultaneously, of strengthening anthropology as a scientific discipline. Communication between societies, difficult as it is, will not suffer – rather the contrary – from the systematic study of the mutual permeability of cultures, that is, the comparison of their different identities.

The six contributions which follow clarify, each in its own way, the various differences between ritual and non-ritual as an indissoluble pair. David Parkin reconsiders Lévi-Strauss's definition of ritual as 'paralanguage' in order better to distance himself from it and relies in particular on the work of Goody and Gerholm to sustain the proposition that rituals 'are not just expressive of abstract ideas but do things, have effects on the world'. He points to what Lewis calls 'the ruling' as distinguished from the 'precise rules' of ritual and suggests that

> Western-trained anthropologists will probably agree as to what a ritual is when they actually see one at work . . . sharing a sense of special occasion that may partly mirror their common epistemology but that is largely shared by the ritual's participants themselves, who heed the 'ruling'.

With this as his starting point, he stresses the directional character of rituals, sorts of passages or voyages through time and space. He proposes the following definition: 'ritual is formulaic spatiality carried out by groups of people who are conscious of its imperative or compulsory nature and who may or may not further inform this spatiality with spoken words'. Even the differences of interpretation among the participants in a ritual are expressed in terms of the movements and directionality of the performance. Parkin insists, in conclusion, that ritual constitutes an obstacle to the natural autonomy of individuals by submitting their bodies to authority the better to place them at the service of society. In reaction, 'human agency . . . develops through its denial to others', which 'is conceptually the opposite of what in Western discourse we conventionally call political agency'. At once 'act' and 'statement', ritual is indeed that 'special occasion' which dramatizes the implicit difference from non-ritual.

Michel Cartry's object is to fulfil the wish expressed by Wittgenstein (1967:246, my translation) 'to trace the lines which connect the shared elements [of all these rites]' and, more specifically, to set forth 'the part [which] is lacking in our vision . . . that which links this picture to our own feelings and thoughts'.[2] He does so by recalling a series of echoes which gradually led him to the discovery of links between the various rituals of a single African society, the Gurmanceba of Burkina Faso. He was guided in his search by the constant recurrence of a song connecting 'two types of initiatory experience', that of novices and that of orphans mourning father or mother. The mourning song of the circumcised leads us to understand that 'the paradigmatic figure of the orphan is the first of the circumcised'. The loss suffered by an orphan rejoins here that 'experienced by the novice being initiated'. The ritual consists in *displacements* which lead both the participants and the anthropologist from one ritual to another, provided that the latter reascends the chain of his surprises until he encounters 'the lines which connect the shared elements so important to Wittgenstein'. Cartry thus elucidates the encounter of two sorts of coherence, that linking the rituals themselves and that governing the anthropologists's criss-cross quest.

With Charles Malamoud we enter the world of India through an analysis of the brother-sister theme both in Vedic myths and in Hindu rituals observable today. He examines the relations between two gods of the Vedic pantheon, Yama and Yamī, whose names mean 'male twin' and 'female twin'. A hymn from the *Rgveda* takes the form of a passionate discussion between Yamī, who ardently desires to unite with her brother, and Yama, who opposes to her arguments the principle of the religious law. It emerges from this dialogue that, while the relation between twin sisters may lead to a sort of coupling (Sky-Earth), the relation between twins of opposite sex requires non-redundancy, the prohibition of incest. In another text, Rākā (the sister of the gods) stitches the seam on man's penis, thus taking care that his procreative faculties not be scattered. The brother-sister pair thus assumes an asymmetrical form which Malamoud discerns in contemporary Hindu rituals as well; indeed, when each year a sister ties a protective thread around her brother's wrist – a service honoured by a payment like the one offered to the officiant in a sacrifice – she is performing a priestly function for him. She spins the thread for his initiation, undoes the knots which tie together the costumes of the bride and bridegroom at his wedding, watches over the ceremony in which his son is given a name (also in return for payment), and receives a coin on the day that nephew eats his first solid food. Malamoud concludes by indicating that, in addition to these rites of passage in which a sister performs priestly services for her brother, there is a feast called 'the second [day] of Yama' in which the brother is offered a bath in his sister's home in commemoration of Yamī's temptation to unite incestuously with her twin. The figure of completeness is no doubt born of the distinction between and the inseparability of the rites performed between brothers and sisters and the success of procreation between husband and wife.

Raymond Jamous considers the relative pertinence of the concepts of 'rite of passage' and 'sacrifice' to an understanding of rituals. His reflections draw sustenance from a case study of the Meo of northern India. 'Rite of passage' puts the accent on the main actor and his transformation, while 'sacrifice' stresses the transformation of a set of asymmetrical relations among the participants in the ritual. In contemporary India, where 'sacrifice is no longer the dominant rite', the study of Meo marriage ceremonies demonstrates that, 'while indeed constituting a rite of passage, [they] are founded primarily on the ritual principles of sacrifice'. The preparatory stages of a marriage – bath, anointment, procession to the forest – are all rites of separation and consecration of the bride and bridegroom which raise them 'above their ordinary condition' like a king and a queen. The marriage ceremonies, viewed as a whole, consist of a succession of ritual services performed by the bridegroom's father's married sister and of ceremonial prestations offered by the bride's mother's brother. When the couple has begotten children, the bridegroom's sister succeeds his father's sister in the performance of these services, while the bride's brother succeeds the mother's brother in offering prestations. Thus the asymmetry between the two sides of a marriage that constitutes the couple persists in new brother-sister relations and highlights the analogy between the gift of a wife and sacrifice; the wife taker is in a superior position, while the marriage and its extensions are situated in the sacrificial logic which contributes to the 'cultural unity of Indian civilization'. Drawing inspiration from the analyses of Malamoud, for whom sacrificial acts 'at once differ radically from actions of profane existence . . . and serve as a model for those actions', Jamous attributes two sorts of effects to rites: as rites of passage they 'separate rite from non-rite', while as sacrifice they 'link rites in terms of the passage of time'.

Building upon his knowledge of the Tobelo of the northern Moluccas and a recent comparative article with C. Barraud, Jos Platenkamp considers rituals the privileged place in which the meaning and value of the morphological relationships that contitute eastern Indonesian societies are articulated in 'transfers of beings and things' that, 'viewed in their totality, constitute systems of circulation'. He attempts to explore what becomes of these systems of circulation when societies are converted to Christianity. If Christian Tobelo ceremonies were to manifest transfers of beings and things similar to those evidenced in the period preceding their conversion and if the church itself appeared to be 'valorized in reference to this [pre-Christian] holistic conceptualization of society', this sort of understanding of rituals would find additional confirmation.

The pre-Christian situation involved 'two interconnected cycles (marriages and first funerals, on the one hand, and second funerals, on the other) and two morphological levels of circulation', within the village and between villages, with the latter level superior to the former in that it brought together the entire society. Throughout these life-death-life cycles, rice and baskets circulated in one direction in exchange for weapons and money circulating in the other. The superior cycle, that of the second funerals, was marked by the circulation of money obtained from the conversion of men and animals that had been killed and ended with a parade of women who acted like warriors overwhelming their enemies. This constituted the transition between the first level and the second, that of marriage relations.

The Tobelo, now Christian, manifest through their ceremonies the existence of two levels: that of marriage, where rice and baskets are exchanged for money and bibles (replacing weapons), and that constituted by two Christian ceremonies held each year. At the end of April, after the rice has been harvested, married women offer plates of rice and baskets to the church to be sold for its benefit, and 'on the first Sunday of January, church prayers are said for the dead . . . each household decorates the graves of its deceased with flowers, whereupon the women, some dressed in military garments, parade through the village'. At this higher level, the church seems to represent both the entire society and the socio-religious whole. The existence of so many similarities between pre-Christian and Christian Tobelo society argues for a method which, by linking the various rites, succeeds in specifying the socio-cosmic task which all of them together perform.

Gerd Baumann, on the basis of his study of the London suburb of Southall, calls into question the unfortunately widespread idea that ritual is 'an act internal to the category or group that celebrates it or celebrates itself through it'. He demonstrates, first of all, that rituals are the product not of unified congregations but of 'competing constituencies'; further, that they not only 'celebrate the perpetuation of social values and self-knowledge' but 'equally speak to aspirations towards cultural change'; and, finally, that rather than being limited to insiders they 'can be "addressed" to "Others", serving to negotiate the differing relationships of . . . participants with these "Others" and in the process reformulate cultural values'. Taking as examples the funeral of a Punjabi murdered by a white and Christmas festivities and birthday parties in Punjabi families living on the outskirts of London, Baumann shows how rituals negotiate relationships between parents, children, and 'invisible Others', 'the English'. In this sense, rituals are 'resources competed for'.

These features are discernible not only in plural but also in non-plural societies and thus prove to be essential characteristics of rituals in general. Baumann identifies five sorts of participants in rituals: bystanders, interested onlookers, guests who one hopes will 'enhance [the ritual's] recognition and status', witnesses who have the power to confer validity on the ritual, and outside beneficiaries. In the Nuba village of Miri in the Sudan, for example, the rain-making ritual brings together members of the community who believe in its efficacy but also many who do not, including the youth of Miri, passing city dwellers, and migrants, who are often fervent Muslims. In conclusion, Baumann suggests that the anthropological distinction between '"us" and "them" is not only contextual but intrinsically dialectical, and this dialectic can be a resource of ritual itself . . . ambiguities may be played out or manipulated, and constituencies may align and realign in the negotiation of who is "us" and who "them."' Thus both communities' comparisons of themselves with others and their efforts to communicate among themselves contribute to the efficacy of rituals. It follows that the domain of rituals is the privileged social arena in which the outlines of countless social relations are shaped.

These six different contributions constitute a reliable sample of present trends in the study of rituals. They have all benefited from the recent achievements of numerous scholars, such as Luc de Heusch, Alfred Gell, Gilbert Lewis, Bruce Kapferer, Jonathan Parry, and Maurice Bloch, which demonstrate that rituals are once again a focus of concern in social anthropology. These scholars all agree in judging essential and consequently problematic the understanding of the difference in each society between ritual and non-ritual. They are in harmony as well in asserting or implying that rituals are at once actions and statements and are, furthermore, all interconnected within a given society.

However, like the social whole of which rituals are an important part, the domain of rituals resists efforts to theorize about and define it. If rituals 'do things,' what exactly does each ritual do, and what do all of them together do, in a given society? Contemporary efforts, even the various attempts to 'deconstruct' rituals, have had a salutary effect: we perceive much better that rituals create and construct, as each society's time unfolds and at varying paces, the social dimension. The fundamental reason that they resist understanding of what they do is that, like the social dimension itself, they are essentially and doubly comparative. The first comparison is internal to each ritual and to the ensemble of the rituals of a given society; it involves expressing the hierarchy of values which orders them, a hierarchy which corresponds to the distinction specific to that society between the indissolubly linked terms of ritual and non-ritual. The second comparison is so thoroughly essential and 'natural' to rituals that anthropological reflection, whose origins are situated at this very point of comparison, seems tempted to neglect it when it is not totally blind to it. This is the comparison between collective identities in terms of the values which rituals illustrate, challenge, and attempt, above all, to order hierarchically. In this comparison between societies, the position accorded rituals in the value hierarchy is itself part of rituals' ongoing task. It is our hope that the various propositions assembled in this book afford anthropology reason to consider that it too is 'natural' and essential – especially in the demanding context of our contemporary world.

NOTES

1 'Une société ne peut ni se créer ni se recréer sans, du même coup, créer de l'idéal. Cette création n'est pas pour elle une sorte d'acte surérogatoire par lequel elle se compléterait, une fois formée; c'est l'acte par lequel elle se fait et refait périodiquement. Aussi, quand on oppose la société idéale à la société réelle comme deux antagon-istes qui nous entraîneraient en des sens contraires, on réalise et on oppose des *abstractions*. La société idéale n'est pas en dehors de la société réelle; elle en fait partie. Bien que nous soyons partagés entre elles comme entre deux pôles qui se repoussent, on ne peut pas tenir

à l'une sans tenir à l'autre. Car une société n'est pas simplement constituée par la masse des individus qui la composent, par le sol qu'ils occupent, par les choses dont ils se servent, par les mouvements qu'ils accomplissent, mais, avant tout, par l'idée qu'elle se fait d'elle-même'.

2 'Linien ziehen, die die gemeinsamen Bestandtelle [aller diesen Riten] verbinden. Es fehlt noch ein Teil der Betrachtung und es ist der, welcher dieses Bild mit unsern eigenen Gefühlen und Gedanken in Verbindung bringt'.

REFERENCES

Dumont, L. (1980) *Homo Hierarchicus: The Caste System and Its Implications*, rev. edn, Chicago: University of Chicago Press.

Durkheim, E. (1925 [1912]) *Les formes élémentaires de la vie réligieuse*, Paris: Alcan.

Wittgenstein, L. (1967) 'Comments on *Golden Bough of Frazer*', *Synthese* 17, 3: 233–53.

Chapter 1

Ritual as spatial direction and bodily division

David Parkin

Lévi-Strauss may be credited with having privileged words, in the form of myth, over ritual, regarded as 'mere' action. One might be forgiven for imagining that he even despised ritual action as being empty of words and that, for him, only myth could give rise to the logocentric reasoning that has allegedly characterized Western forms of rationality. For example, he is charged with regarding ritual as 'the bastardisation of thought' (Crick 1982: 300, citing de Heusch 1980), with thought itself being most imaginatively expressed in myth. It is not unreasonable to infer that, for Lévi-Strauss, action without words, including for example exchanges of goods and services and those entailed in marriage, *is* the most elementary form of communication and, despite the use elsewhere of the action-based metaphor *bricolage* to characterize mythological thought, myth is the highest (Lévi-Strauss 1966: 16–33). In his own words,

> The value of the ritual as meaning seems to reside in instruments and gestures: it is a *paralanguage*. The myth, on the other hand, manifests itself as a *metalanguage*; it makes full use of discourses, but does so by situating its own significant oppositions at a higher level of complexity than that required by language operating for profane ends.
>
> (Lévi-Strauss 1977 [1973]: 66)

I wish to suggest that the manner in which many anthropologists, including Lévi-Strauss, have understood ritual entitles us to reverse this privileging and to argue that it is precisely because ritual is fundamentally made up of physical action, with words often only optional or arbitrarily replaceable, that it can be regarded as having a distinctive potential for performative imagination that is not reducible to verbal assertions.

Since Lévi-Strauss's early major impact there has developed a now widespread anthropological view that words and actions are inseparably inscribed in each other: 'language penetrates the social' (Ardener 1982: 12). However, to go back to the unstudied counter-implications of Tambiah's (1968) pioneering analysis of the magical power of words, the claim that speech can stand alone in certain situations as autonomously efficacious and as having illocutionary effect (and so constituting action) obliges us also to consider the alternative possibility of a world of non-words or, at least, of actions which achieve their legitimacy through performance including speech only secondarily, if at all.

I would certainly agree that the linguistic is inseparably part of the social and that speech is itself a form of social action – a view developed long ago through the work on propositions of Austin (1962), Searle (1969), and others, as well as, from a somewhat different perspective, the later Wittgenstein. I imagine also that few would dissent from the claim that this inseparability of word and deed characterizes a prevalent and sometimes reflexive anthropological view of social process. But I would suggest that anthropological ideas of ritual contrasted with myth constantly threaten to reverse this premise: it is often part of the alleged special character of ritual that it *does* presuppose an action or series of actions which does not need speech. Thus, while myth is rendered as privileging words, ritual is held to privilege physical action; but it is an action that can only be understood as bodily movement towards or positioning with respect to other bodily movements and positions. If such movements are a principal feature of ritual, then it must be through them rather than through verbal assertions that people make their main statements.

An implication of this view is that all rituals are in some way rites of passage: in other words, that they presuppose phasal movement, directionality, and positioning. Since it is through such movements and positions that participants make statements both about the world and about the ritual itself, a further implication is that there may often arise a quality which keeps the ritual going and which I will call 'agency by default': that is to say, it is less that persons opt to set up and maintain these rituals than that, in criticizing others' competence in bodily movement and direction, they may be left with the task of organizing the ritual. This agency by default is the underside of the now familiar claim, advanced earlier by Leach (1954), Southall (1954), and Middleton (1960), that rivals compete to control the conduct of rituals in order to legitimate leadership roles.

But what is here meant by a ritual, or by ritual in general? It would be tedious to go through yet again the lists of criteria by which they have been laboriously defined. There have been valiant attempts, although it is amazing how nominalist they can be, with the most satisfactory understandings of purported ritual being drawn not from definitional criteria but from extended case studies. There is, however, an approach which hovers over the assumption that rituals are always in some way regarded as rites of passage and that they survive through agency by default. It is an approach which sits uneasily with those other approaches which have been variously dubbed functionalist, intellectualist, symbolist, and Marxist. Rather than give it a name, let me outline its overlapping features:

We can take as encompassing a time-span during which this approach has emerged two little-known articles: one by Jack Goody (1977) and the other by Thomas Gerholm (1988). Goody's 'Against "Ritual"' is a witty deconstruction of the concept, insisting that it can never satisfactorily be defined. It concludes with a somewhat whimsical appeal to see ritual within 'a hierarchy of organised skills and processes' which include formal, repetitive behaviour, Goffmanesque small encounters, and large-scale ceremonies. Gerholm's paper also deconstructs current assumptions of ritual, but, whereas Goody's dismantles in order to rebuild a broader sociological edifice of interaction, it suggests that ritual is anything but an edifice and that it is an arena of contradictory and contestable perspectives – participants having their own reasons, viewpoints, and motives and in fact is made up as it goes along. Not surprisingly, Gerholm calls this a post-modernist view, but he is certainly not wedded to this label.

His example is the description by V. S. Naipaul in *The Enigma of Arrival* (1987) of his sister's funeral in Trinidad, where people of Indian Hindu extraction constitute a large minority (40 per cent) coexisting with others of European, African, and Chinese descent and with adherents of other religions, including Christianity. On hearing of his sister's death, Naipaul does not immediately depart for Trinidad but mourns privately in Britain where he lives. When he does arrive at his family home in Trinidad, he is amazed by what he sees. There is an insistence that the woman be given a 'proper' Hindu funerary ritual, for which the dead girl's brother summons a Hindu 'priest' who, throughout the ceremony, is questioned by the brother as to the meaning of actions in the ritual. We are given the impression that the priest himself interprets his scriptures very liberally and hesitantly. Naipaul asks whether anything quite like this ritual has occurred before.

Gerholm's purpose in providing this outline is to suggest that such jumbled-up ritual is a common feature of the modern world, in which, like Naipaul, we can be in London one day, sorrowfully meditating on a sister's death, and next day have flown the many thousands of miles to attend the funeral, slipping almost unnoticed into the melée. He also argues that, while this may for us as anthropologists be an extreme case of fragmented ritual, that of Victor Turner's superinformant, Muchona, with his description of ritual as made up of artful internal logic and consistency, may well be an equally extreme case of coherence (Turner 1959). I suspect that fragmentation of meaning is always produced but is dispersed in different ways: in so-called isolated and homogeneous cultures, its dispersal may take the form of spatially as well as temporally opposed whole rituals (e.g., funerals in one area or era may invert the forms of funerals but resemble those of, say, weddings in another area or time), while in so-called exposed, heterogeneous cultures, the dispersal or fragmentation may occur within the ritual.

Gerholm does not wish, however, to remain with the idea of ritual as only dispersing meaning. He argues in favour of an intellectualist rather than symbolist perspective: that rituals, however they are defined, are not just expressive of abstract ideas but do things, have effects on the world, and are work that is carried out – that they are indeed performances. This expressively instrumental view of ritual is certainly that which has gained currency over the last decade, as is evident, say, from Gilbert Lewis's study of the Gnau of New Guinea in 1980 to Bloch's 1986 analysis of Merina circumcision ritual and others since.

A key notion in this development is what Lewis calls the 'ruling' (1980: 11). Participants in a ritual may well contest the proper conduct of the ceremony or may acknowledge their ignorance and ask others what to do or what some action or object means. But that the ritual *is* a ritual and is supposed to follow some time-hallowed precedent in order to be effective or simply to be a proper performance is not in question. An implication of Lewis's study is that Western-trained anthropologists will probably agree as to what a ritual is when they actually see one at work (1980: 8, 14), sharing a sense of special occasion that may partly mirror their common epistemology but that is also largely shared by the ritual's participants themselves, who heed the 'ruling'.

We can see this as more than just custom, for the sense of occasion that makes up ritual calls for 'public attention' (Lewis 1980: 7, 20–21) in a way that custom, if carried out 'correctly', does not. Lewis tends to regard ritual and custom as drawing on similar attributes (1980: 11–13), but let me here make a distinction between them that is consistent with his emphasis on the 'alerting' quality of ritual. Custom is silent and, if properly carried out, unnoticed: it is only when the customary greeting is impaired or the man orders his drink in an odd way that the custom is noticed in its breach. As the obverse, ritual is culturally loud and vibrant even when acoustically mute and tranquil: the sacrifice, initiation, or May Day parade is already a publicly marked event, even when carried out behind closed doors or secretly; whether or not it is deemed to have gone wrong is part of the putative public gaze which constitutes it. Excluded from this definition then, are personal rituals which may anticipate the myth-dreams of collective cults but which, as private secrets, do not yet evoke public judgement.

The emphasis on 'ruling', then, is an invitation to us as outside observers not to record or decipher precisely sequenced rules but rather to acknowledge that people expect there to be rules as a condition of public ritual. In other words, even when neither observers nor participants can agree on, understand, or even perceive ritual regulations, they are united by a sense of the occasion as being in some way rule-governed and as necessarily so in order to be complete, efficacious, and proper.

So-called structuralist approaches to ritual have, of course, stressed precisely the logic of this rule-governed behaviour and have in fact sought the regularities that transcend the individual consciousness of participants. Recent work by de Heusch (1985) on sacrifice, by Tcherkezoff (1983) on Nyamwezi dualism, and by Werbner (1989) on his own and others' ethnography are examples. Such scholars see themselves as tackling the challenge thrown to structuralism to account for history and agency in the decoding of cultural logic(s). Applause for their ingenuity is, however, tempered by reservations about the temptation in structuralism to enter into infinite regress in the discovery, or creation, of new structures. For my purposes, however, I do not wish to set up structuralist against such other approaches as intellectualism and symbolism. Rather, what interests me is the use made, in such studies, of directionality – of axes, cardinal points, concentric zones, and other expressions of spatial orientation and movement. Werbner's most recent study is in fact entitled *Ritual Passage, Sacred Journey* and includes essays which justify the title.

My own division would be between two approaches: (1) that which tends to treat ritual as a process of such internal conceptual significance, if not consistency, that we are given only a limited idea of that ritual's movement through social space and (2) that which, instead, emphasizes the ritual as clearly concerned with directionality and as making up a journey or passage undertaken and/or marked by participants standing in spatial relationships to each other. (Perhaps these are emphases rather than approaches, for they are often found within the same analysis.)

The approach to ritual as always concerned with movement, directionality, and spatial orientation is, I think, distinctive. It takes up a hint from V. Turner (1982: 24) that all rituals are, in a way, rites of passage, including both those that celebrate birth, initiation, marriage, death, and seasonal changes and those he calls rites of affliction. We can extend the list to include the many liturgical rituals occurring in the annual calendars of so-called world religions. They all, following Turner following Van Gennep, involve a liminal phase, a betwixt-and-between element, and so presuppose an initial phase of separation and one of reaggregation. Can we think of any ritual which does not have such phases, however much they may be redefined (see T. Turner 1977)? The more specific use of metaphors of passage and journeying is also, of course, found in many descriptions of, say, Amazonian shamanism (Descola 1992, Overing 1990), African divination (Parkin 1979; 1991), marriage ceremonies premised on ideas of capture, elopement, and reciprocal visiting, funerary rituals involving the carrying, burial, and sometimes reburial of corpses (Bloch 1971; Feeley-Harnik 1991), special processions, and pilgrimages (Sallnow 1987).

I want to go farther than this and suggest that it is precisely the infinite combinatorial possibilities for directional change and spatial orientation that almost merge ritual with art and yet also, in conjunction with its purposive nature, make it not just performative but performative-for-some-goal and for-someone. If I may be allowed to impose a Western-derived distinction, art tends towards a performative *en-soi*, culminating ultimately in the magical and aesthetic power of directionally oriented and shaped objects (so-called fetishes), while ritual tends towards a performative *pour-soi*, conscious, through its participants, of its power to make or break life depending on the directions and, literally, the steps it takes and so entrusted with that good faith, yet forever experimenting with these spatial forms. Changes in the steps, dances, movements, gestures, spaces, axes, and directions of ritual can never be neutral if noticed, for they deviate from a pre-existing form remembered or constructed by at least some participants and/or onlookers. And while public deviation in ritual threatens the ritual and is, indeed, its inner contradiction, it is also that which sustains it, for disagreements over ritual procedure hold public attention. Much the same may be said about claims to the sanctity of any words used in the ritual. Words may be important elements of ritual performance, sometimes critically so. But while words may stand alone in myth unaccompanied by gesture, they are dependent on the directional movements that make up ritual. It is in this sense that ritual, full of spatial movement and gestural performance, could make the evolutionary transition to drama and theatre, based at first primarily on mime rather than on dialogue.

With such steps and movements, rather than the words, as the main points of articulation in ritual, it is not surprising that it is these directional and spatial qualities which are commonly referred to as the basis of the 'proper', 'hallowed', and 'effective' ritual. I have never come across a ritual in which the spatial movements and orientation counted for nothing and the words were all-important. By contrast, I have never met a ritual in which the words, though sometimes claimed to be essential for proper performance, were not inscribed in spatially arranged phases and sequences: it is less that their utterance heralded a new phase than that certain points and places in the ritual process were chosen as appropriate niches for verbal expression. It might be argued that certain kinds of silent prayer are exceptions to this generalization, but, even so, they commonly assume bodily and directional postures, such as facing an altar or Mecca, such that even the silent prayers permitted to individuals absent from a mosque or church may be regarded as a temporary and spatially expedient variant of the more desirable public and collective ritual act carried out in a house of worship.

At this point let me offer a minimal definition of ritual: Ritual is formulaic spatiality carried out by groups of people who are conscious of its imperative or compulsory nature and who may or may not further inform this spatiality with spoken words.

Definitions are risky adventures, and this attempt seeks both to summarize my argument so far and to avoid the teleological pitfall of claiming that repetitive, formalized activities without words are ritual while words without action are myth. I draw on an unorthodox view of 'proposition' as sometimes communicated through silent, physical movement and not through words (Parkin 1980: 48) and so agree with Lewis (1980), Tambiah (1968), Rappaport (1979), and especially Bloch (1986: 195) that ritual is neither fully a statement nor fully an action – for it is indeed the case that a ritual need not fulfill a stated aim in order to continue and be believed in. But what I do regard as fundamental to this ambiguity and tension between a ritual's performance and assertion is its formulaic spatiality, namely, the capacity to create and act through idioms of passage, movement, including exchange, journey, axis, concentricism, and up-and-down directions.

Just as the language of anthropological theory is based on metaphors of spatial direction, progress, and conquest (Salmond 1982), so rituals can only be described, by either observers or participants, as movements between points and places and as positionings. But this formulaic spatiality is not uncontested. Indeed, I would argue that for rituals in particular, and for rituals in general, there must be contestation. Why should this be so? Here we return to the view of ritual as concerned with the idea of ruling or rule-governedness, even when people consistently dispute precise rules of procedure.

The very paucity or incompleteness of verbal description in ritual and, as in written liturgies, the infinite possibilities offered for interpretation render questions about the meaning of spatial direction and patterning vague and ambiguous. In our fieldwork we never expect nowadays to see a ritual repeated in precisely the same manner, however much some of our informants may insist on standardization. It was a problem of positivism in its heyday to seek a 'proper' or *Ur*-form from which other forms had deviated. But while some of the participants in a ritual may well insist on the possibility of exact ritual replication, others are likely to see error and confusion in the conduct of a ritual. The standardizers and the disputants reproduce our own epistemological differences: between those seeking true representation in the correct reproduction of ritual and other events and those wrestling with the paradox of family resemblances between successive rituals (all recognizably covered by Lewis's idea of the 'ruling') coexisting with the fact that rituals are also always partly being made up as they are carried out.

This paradox of the apparent blueprint and evident on-the-spot inventiveness has raised the question, also, of what we mean by ritual specialist knowledge. Of course, elders, priests, and others may still be referred to by people as their ritual experts. But when, as Gerholm observed with reference to Naipaul's account, the priest is clearly not, and cannot be, the consistent source of ritual wisdom that some would consider him, it is no longer surprising that inconsistencies in ritual performance and in statement are not papered over but simply left as they are: unanswered and probably unasked questions.

This fallibility in ritual knowledge is well brought out by Fardon (1991), who shows how, within a single cultural group, one regional ritual specialist regards his own knowledge as limited and probably wrong when compared with that of ritual experts in an allegedly more autochthonous area yet remains a ritual practitioner. Once again, the ritual ruling rather than the precise rules, meanings, and effects is what constitutes recognition of the knowledge.

When we apply this notion that ritual knowledge is made up of overlapping partial 'truths' and partial 'falsehoods' to the conduct of rituals, we see why an idea of formulaic spatiality is so important. The formulaic evokes its opposite. Ritually 'proper' spaces, positions, and directions may be prescribed by those in authority, but individuals can slip, if only slightly and gradually, beyond boundaries and can widen, narrow, or shift these spatial orientations. Like Marilyn Strathern's Mount Hagen co-wives who subvert husbands' authority not verbally but silently through covert actions and underperformance in marriage (1972: 314), ritual participants can, in moments of ritual enthusiasm and emotion, spatially reshape the passage of the ritual, blurring the boundaries between phases, groups, and activities. Those in charge of the ritual may scold and insist on proper reordering, but, if a growing number of ritual participants take the new direction, such officials may instead tacitly accept the spatial shift and even claim it as the 'real way' – allowing new agency by default.

At this point, such abstract description can usefully be fleshed out through ethnographic example. I take the case of burials and funerals among some peoples of the Kenya coast, but I believe that comparable cases could be made for rituals of birth, initiation, naming, and marriage, as well as for the cleansing rites of affliction and of rain-making.

The Kenya coast has three ecological zones: cattle-keeping in the dry western hinterland, cash-crop and subsistence farming inland but nearer the eastern coast, and fishing along the eastern coast itself, out into the Indian Ocean. The hinterland cattle-keeping people are regarded and regard themselves as 'pure' Giriama and as practising and knowing the 'purest' Giriama versions of ritual; the intermediary, agricultural people are regarded and regard themselves as less knowledgeable about such ritual and as threatened by non-Giriama influences on the coast, where Islam and, increasingly, Christianity have a strong hold.

There does appear to me to be more consistency in burial and funerary practice in the 'pure' western cattle-keeping hinterland. Both men and women are buried on their right sides, with their feet pointing to the west and their eyes to a legendary point of migratory origin. The burial is followed by a seven-day funeral, and some three or four months afterwards there is a second funeral of three days for women and four for men. Few practices deviate from this spatial pattern and from others I have not described.

Thirty kilometres to the east, in the agricultural zone of coconut palms, cashew trees, and maize, people broadly follow this pattern, but there are important exceptions. First, Christians may insist that prayers be said for the body once it is in the grave, while non-Christians insist that its passage from its house to the grave, that is, from this world to that of the ancestors, must be immediate and therefore try to cover the body with earth quickly. If Christians can cluster in sufficient strength round the grave, they can delay the covering-up of the body and say Christian prayers, but this depends on their assuming prominent positions in the cortège by slipping in front of customarily more eligible pallbearers and processionists. Second, some participants may try to have a man's body buried on its right side and a woman's on its left, these being the respective positions adopted during sexual intercourse – a change that would preserve the customary demand that the eyes face north but would reverse for women the directional positions of the head and feet. Were women's bodies to undergo this reversal of position, Giriama burial practice would show similarities with that of some other, closely related peoples in this densely populated area, thus compromising the distinctiveness of Giriama cultural identity. Again, some participants make no mention of the direction in which the eyes should face and instead claim that the body's head should face east because that is where the sea is or that the feet (or head) should face west because that it where a more recent sacred origin is. Still others, influenced by Islam, claim that the eastern or north-eastern direction (depending on where the funeral is held) is significant because it points to Mecca (Parkin 1991: 133–4).

These very few examples alone (and there are many more) show the importance of spatial orientation among a section of people whose high population density and slight ethnic intermingling result from cash-cropping, and indicate how new agents and partial ritual authorities may come and go through default as well as though personal ambition.

As we move to the third ecological area, the coast itself, heavily influenced by Islam, these complexities of spatial direction and position are compounded still further. As well as the above, there are differences which result from the fact that members of a homestead or of a dispersed family may include Muslims and non-Muslims and perhaps Christians as well. Although a body will be buried in only one homestead (for there is never removal and reinterment), another funeral (and sometimes even more than one) may be held by members of a competing religious group, usually simultaneously in another homestead, either that of a separately residing brother or that of someone to whom the deceased's father or mother, say, was linked. The same spatial separation may characterize second funerals or wakes, in addition to there being possible differences of timing, conduct, and duration. Muslim ceremonies, for instance, are shorter, less lavish, and sometimes followed much sooner by the second funeral.

My argument is that, however much participants in a ritual may dispute and debate the significance, meaning, and propriety of ritual behaviour, using words to great effect in doing so, they can only demonstrate the saliency, success, and effectiveness of what they have to say through performative practice, and issues of spatial orientation and position are the only means at their disposal, being fundamentally constitutive of the ritual itself.

This might seem to apply most obviously to funerals, which, of all the conventional rites of passage, seem the most directly concerned with proper spatial ordering and orientation, whether through Hertzian concepts of life, death, and the right and left hands or through the very movement and direction taken by the corpse. Such an assumption, however, imposes too literal an understanding of spatial orientation and direction. We must look at spatial usage not only literally but metaphorically. After all, the very notion of the rite of passage was as much a metaphorical insight as a literal description of physical movement. It connotes social and cosmological as well as physical direction.

This approach allows us to extend the spatial idea of ritual to the human body itself, which, as well as sometimes physically being moved, can be regarded as subject to journeys and passages even when it remains in one position. I have spoken already of the use of bodily journeying in divination and shamanism: sometimes the body of the person as a whole is believed to travel, but sometimes, as in Giriama divination, the diviner speaks of a journey from the head to the heart via the liver, kidneys, back, and legs, dwelling on each bodily part as a possible stage in an illness or as an allegory of misfortune.

We touch here on the widely reported phenomenon of bodily partition. Among many peoples, the skulls of the buried bodies of all or of key persons may later be moved to other areas. Some peoples remove a number of limbs also, each being taken in a specific direction to a specific place.

Circumcision, clitoridectomy, and the disposal and sometimes burial of the placenta and/or umbilical cord all indicate further the propensity in key rituals for body division and separation to occur. The very idea behind the rite of passage as classically reported by Van Gennep (1960 [1909]) and, later, Richards (1956) is that it changes the total person, including the nature and destiny of his or her body. The sexual, reproductive, emotional, intellectual, and role changes resulting from the *chisungu* female initiation rite among the Bemba are themselves attendant on the community's intervening and trying to influence the autonomous changes that accompany bodily maturation: the community cuts, divides, and reorders the mature body's faculties so that, from the viewpoint of authority, they may be better placed to serve society. In this authoritative tendency to divide the body and spatially relocate it in a conjoined metaphorical and literal sense I think we see ritual as a gloss on the problem of personal human agency. Whether at puberty, marriage, or death, the individual body threatens to join the autonomous worlds of mature adults or ancestors. Its redirection and reassembly by those in power, claiming to act on behalf of the community, curb that autonomy.

In pointing up the possibilities for bodily dispersion, we see in ritual a constant reminder of the fact that political control over persons is as much a physical as an intellectual exercise. There is perhaps a Cartesian tendency in Western thinking to privilege control over the intellect: you can destroy my body but, with forbearance, I will keep from you the destruction of my mind. But the mind cannot function without the body, and the composite non-dualist view of the person as inseparably both mind and body and as vulnerable as a totality is what seems most stressed in ritual.

Formulaic spatiality and the contestability provoked by it thus inform the actual places and directions taken by ritual performance, the metaphorical drama of journey and passage in the performance, and the way in which bodies and minds of participants will be allocated and distributed physically as well as metaphorically. Perhaps it is only through ritual that humans will collude collectively in their own movement, transformation, dispersion, and partition. I would even go so far as to suggest that, through ritual, people set up what I have called 'tangled states' (1979; 1991) – spatial and bodily states of confusion, admixture, and complexity – which they then seek to disentangle. Through such disentanglement, people reimpose order on themselves and on the parts and places that make them up. These tangled states are not, I imagine, calculated in advance. Rather, they arise when participants interfere in each other's interpretations of the ritual 'ruling'. Human agency here, then, develops through its denial to others: it is the denial of the other that, by default, promotes the self. This is conceptually the opposite of what in Western discourse we conventionally call political agency, according to which persons consciously strive to achieve position through a prior and dominant idea of self-determination and self-promotion.

REFERENCES

Ardener, E. (1982) 'Social anthropology, language, and reality', in D. Parkin (ed.) *Semantic Anthropology*, ASA Monograph 22, London: Tavistock.

Austin, J. L. (1962) *How to Do Things with Words*, Oxford: Oxford University Press.

Bloch, M. (1971) *Placing the Dead*, London: Seminar Press.

—— (1986) *From Blessing to Violence: History and Ideology in the Circumcision Ritual of the Merina of Madagascar*, Cambridge: Cambridge University Press.

Crick, M. (1982) 'The anthropology of knowledge', *Annual Reviews in Anthropology* 11: 287–313.

de Heusch, L. (1985) 'Physiology and cosmogony: rites de passage among the Thonga', in I. Karp and C. S. Bird (eds) *Explorations in African Systems of Thought*, Bloomington: Indiana University Press.

Descola, P. (1992) 'Societies of nature and the nature of society', in A. Kuper (ed.) *Conceptualizing society*, London: Routledge.

Fardon, R. (1991) *Between God, the Dead, and the Wild*, London: Edinburgh University Press/Washington, D.C.: Smithsonian Institution Press.

Feeley-Harnik, G. (1991) *A Green Estate: Restoring Independence in Madagascar*, Washington, D.C., and London: Smithsonian Institution Press.

Gerholm, T. (1988) 'On ritual: a post-modernist view', *Ethnos* 3–4: 190–203.

Goody, J. (1977) 'Against "ritual": loosely structured thoughts on a loosely defined topic', in S. F. Moore and B. G. Myerhoff (eds) *Secular Ritual*, Assen and Amsterdam: Van Gorcum.

Leach, E. (1954) *Political Systems of Highland Burma*, London: Bell.

Lévi-Strauss, C. (1966) *The Savage Mind*, London: Weidenfeld and Nicolson.

—— (1977) *Structural Anthropology 2*, London: Allen Lane.

Lewis, G. (1980) *Day of Shining Red: An Essay in Understanding Ritual*, Cambridge: Cambridge University Press.

Middleton, J. (1960) *Lugbara Religion*, London: Oxford University Press for the International African Institute.

Naipaul, V. S. (1987) *The Enigma of Arrival*, New York: Knopf.

Overing, J. (1990) 'The shaman as a maker of worlds: Nelson Goodman in the Amazon', *Man*, n.s., 25: 602–19.

Parkin, D. (1979) 'Straightening the paths from wilderness: the case of divinatory speech', *Journal of the Anthropological Society of Oxford* 10: 147–60.

——— (1980) 'The creativity of abuse,' *Man*, n.s., 15: 45–64.

——— (1991) *Sacred Void: Spatial Images of Work and Ritual among the Giriama of Kenya*, Cambridge: Cambridge University Press.

Rappaport, R. A. (1979) 'The obvious aspects of ritual', in *Ecology, Meaning, and Religion*, Berkeley: North Atlantic Books.

Richards, A. I. (1956) Chisungu: *A Girls' Initiation Ceremony among the Bemba of Northern Rhodesia*, London: Faber and Faber.

Sallnow, M. J. (1987) *Pilgrims of the Andes: Regional Cults in Cusco*, Washington, D.C.: Smithsonian Institution Press.

Salmond, A. (1982) 'Theoretical landscapes', in D. Parkin (ed.) *Semantic Anthropology*, ASA Monograph 22, London: Tavistock.

Searle, J. R. (1969) *Speech Acts*, Cambridge: Cambridge University Press.

Southall, A. W. (1954) *Alur Society*, Cambridge: Heffer.

Strathern, M. (1972) *Women in Between: Female Roles in a Male World*, London: Seminar (Academic) Press.

Tambiah, S. J. (1968) 'The magical power of words', *Man*, n.s., 3: 175–208.

Tcherkezoff, S. (1983) *Le roi nyamwezi: La droite et la gauche*, Cambridge: Cambridge University Press/Paris: Editions de la Maison des Sciences de l'Homme.

Turner, T. (1977) 'Transformation, hierarchy, and transcendence: a reformulation of Van Gennep's model of the structure of rites de passage', in S. F. Moore and B. G. Myerhoff (eds) *Secular Ritual*, Assen and Amsterdam: Van Gorcum.

Turner, V. W. (1959) 'Muchona the hornet, interpreter of religion', in J. Casagrande (ed.) *In the Company of Men*, New York: Harper.

——— (1982) *From Ritual to Theatre: The Human Seriousness of Play*, New York: Performing Arts Journal Publications.

Van Gennep, A. (1960 [1909]) *The Rites of Passage*, trans. M. B. Vizedom and G. L. Cafee, Chicago: University of Chicago Press.

Werbner, R. (1989) *Ritual Passage, Sacred Journey: The Process and Organization of Religious Movement*, Washington, D.C.: Smithsonian Institution Press.

Chapter 2

From one rite to another: the memory in ritual and the ethnologist's recollection

Michel Cartry

In his 'Remarks on Frazer's *Golden Bough*', Wittgenstein (1982: 28) writes of the comparative study of rites, 'The most striking thing seems to me to be, beyond all the similarities, the diversity of all these rites. There is a multiplicity of faces with common features continually reappearing here and there'. I will focus on this question of the multiplicity of reappearances of common features from one rite to another, attempting to structure it by confining myself to two segments of distinct ceremonies that I observed among the Gurmanceba (Gurma, Gourmantché) of Burkina Faso.

Wittgenstein continues, 'What one would like to do is trace the lines linking common components'. For ethnologists, it is a commonplace that many features recur in the various ceremonies performed by a given society, but what I am trying to discover is the 'lines' that can be drawn from one rite to another in a society's ritual. How is one to reconstruct from these features a composition that takes multiple linkages into account?

As we go on reading Wittgenstein, an additional difficulty crops up, one that ethnologists, in particular, must confront during every phase of their work. The passage ends as follows: 'A part is still missing in our vision of things, the part connecting this vision with our own feelings and thoughts. This is the part that gives things depth'. To put Wittgenstein's proposition to the test, I tried to recall occasions during fieldwork among the Gurmanceba when, during a ceremony, it occured to me that the segment of a ceremony being performed before me might be connected to a segment of a previously observed ceremony of a different sort. Through this effort at recollection, I identified several representative cases with regard to the positions which the observer and the object observed may occupy in this type of experience.

The first and simplest case is 'It means nothing to me'. I am observing a ceremony which involves singing and dancing. Suddenly my attention is drawn to a dance step and the accompanying rhythmic figure. Although I feel as though I had already seen this step or heard this figure, I am unable to recall the occasion. What kind of ceremony was being celebrated? I think of asking the people around me, but no precise question comes to mind. I tell myself, 'There's no such thing as an unlimited repertoire. Here as everywhere else, some figures recur freely without thereby acquiring any particular meaning'. At the moment, 'It means nothing to me'.

Another representative case may be called 'It reminds me of something, but . . . ' I am watching the *kululi* ('casting out death') rite that ends the funeral ceremony to which certain elderly persons are entitled. The burial took place several weeks ago, but today the tomb is being rebuilt and the deceased's relatives have placed all sorts of objects on it. It is clear that we are dealing with an exposition rite. The objects are not viaticums for the deceased but have been placed there to be seen at leisure by the mourners who will come at sunset and crowd around the tomb to watch his eldest son and daughter dance for their father (who is thought to be watching as well). Among these objects are a spear stuck in the ground, around which are twisted branches of shea tree leaves, and, near it, tufts of cotton and a metal bar normally used by women for carding cotton but here integrated into the rite as a musical instrument, used to strike a little water drum in rhythm.

My informant is beside me, and I ask him about the cotton. He tells me, as if it were obvious, that 'it is the sperm of the father who made the child' and that 'one also puts cotton in the lying-in room'. I have indeed observed the latter for myself, but at the time I thought I was aware of all sorts of reasons for cotton to be placed, as an object witness, in the lying-in room. Now, however, the cotton representing sperm brings a sense of the other fluids which are present at the funeral scene – the milk of the shea tree leaves, the amniotic fluid of the water drums. Birth objects are present at the scene of the funeral. This does indeed say something to me, but is this reminder of birth at the moment of death more than trivial?

In a third case, 'I don't understand what's going on'. Here I am puzzled by an object that is present during a ceremony performed in the enclosure where boys are initiated. I have already learnt many things about the meaning of what the recently circumcised boys are wearing in the way of clothes and accessories (cotton squares worn as loincloths but tied in a way reminiscent of the cotton band with which young girls adorn themselves to veil their nudity, a linen bag slung over the shoulders in which various objects are kept, etc.). I see these things and the staffs that they carry as adjuncts to the body. Two of these staffs are carried by each novice. I am already aware that the novices are joined together in twin couples, and I know too that the placenta, dealt with in a very sophisticated way, is the newborn's twin. Furthermore, I remember having seen a few staffs at birth rites.

Although I do not ask my informant for further elucidation, given that I am already overwhelmed by his way of treating the number two, he announces as if it were obvious that one of the staffs at the boys' initiation is associated with the baby's 'second', which is the placenta. In this veritable inflation of symbolism, I might in fact try to discover multiple series of relations between birth rites and boys' initiation rites, but this aspect of things has no attraction because it does not erase my first impression that, for the time being, 'I don't understand what's going on'.

I have of course deliberately presented the above as a mild caricature of what an ethnologist, keenly looking for anything that might form a connection between the ritual, his feelings, and his thoughts, might grasp from his observation post. It is from this vantage point that I will attempt to characterize the lines linking one rite to another to which Wittgenstein refers.

In a fine essay about how rites are organized, Pierre Smith (1979) has dealt with the sort of problem I have in mind, and I shall borrow one of his ideas. Hypothesizing that several 'ritual systems' coexist within a single culture, he has inquired into the nature of the links between the rites that compose a single ritual system. He has maintained that such rites 'correspond to or contrast with each other, complete or repeat each other, in more obvious ways, in every respect, than those linked to' other ritual systems (p. 145). To classify the various ritual systems coexisting within a single culture, he has taken as a criterion the nature of the circumstances determining their occurrence (e.g., whether or not they refer to a natural cycle, whether they concern the group or the individual). I am not sure that his criteria for classifying rites are always pertinent (for instance, it seems somewhat artificial to arrange rites according to whether they are occasional or periodic), but this is not the point I want to make here. What I want to borrow from his essay is the idea that if acts (or segments of acts) from two different ceremonies do correspond, then we must postulate the existence of an operator to ensure the co-ordination of the whole – an operator which would be the ritual itself. Smith quotes a famous passage from *Mythologiques* in which Lévi-Strauss (1971: 577–96) notes the many similarities in internal organization between a myth and a piece of music. Although Smith stresses the innovative character of this comparison, one gets the feeling that what he would really have liked to have seen compared is the organization of a piece of music and that of a ritual.

Viewed in this light, Smith's idea takes on new meaning. When he says that rites correspond to each other he is not just rehashing the commonplace that, in a ritual system, as in the systems studied by linguists, each element can be defined only in terms of its relations (of equivalence or opposition) with others. Beyond this, he leads the reader to wonder whether the form resulting from the interdependence of the elements in a ritual is not analogous to the form that links the parts, or voices, of a musical score.

I began by describing a few field observations that have been left hanging, at least with regard to the question of how to relate distinct rites which present similar features. I would now like to offer a further observation which, I hope, will not be left hanging. I watched a certain segment of the funeral ceremony several times in various villages and with different actors. When I saw it for the *n*th time, I realized that something was happening which seemed intended to recall another rite. This something was not a dance step, and it did not involve an object; it was a song, and not the music but the words. It was the words that recalled another rite. Of course, words, because they convey an immediate meaning, do not serve as a reminder in the same way that objects do. When I first made this observation I did not, I think, distinctly perceive what was at issue. I shall return to this moment when the song that I had heard before began meaning something new to me – a moment I shall henceforth refer to as my 'reference observation' – once I have described the context of the ritual segment in question.

During the dry season in a Gurmanceba village, mourning songs, performed by women, can be heard almost every evening from one compound or another. The visitor soon learns that this performance is part of the ritual obligations incumbent on a family for a kinsperson who has the rank of elder. In this type of funeral mourning begins on the day of burial and continues until the actual funeral ceremony, when the most memorable rite, the aforementioned 'casting out death', takes place. Throughout this period of several weeks or even months, the following rite is performed every evening for the deceased's family: At nightfall, women relatives gather in the compound's inner courtyard and, for about two hours, sing mourning songs from the *ku-yaani* (songs of death) series while the deceased supposedly comes back to occupy his room, whose door has been left open. His wives are not allowed to be part of the group of singers because this rite involves a sort of quarantine for them. If the funeral is for an old woman, a like isolation is imposed on her husband.

In these songs, the most recurrent themes are the ineluctability of death, the suffering of bereavement, and the grief of those closest to the deceased, in particular the chill that settles upon them. Some of the songs also evoke the weary path that the deceased must follow before reaching the land of the ancestors; the water drum used to accompany them beats out the rhythm of his steps. The last song in the series, however, contrasts with these songs in its content and form and in the motions associated with it.

Prior to my reference observation, this song, called *bu'mpo*, had already attracted my attention for three reasons. First, it was performed by the deceased's eldest daughter with a mime that made the audience laugh. Secondly, it had a scansion effect during this nighttime ceremony, since it signalled the end of one part and the beginning of another; once its last words were sung, the deceased's daughter abruptly left the compound to 'refresh' her father's grave in the outer courtyard. Thirdly, the words, instead of dwelling on grief, referred to initiation.

Had the song intrigued me enough to focus upon it, I might have had the opportunity to ponder a well-known property of funeral ceremonies, namely, that they often enact scenes that link death to initiation. I might have tried to see whether the Gurmanceba conception of this linkage had led them to create an original model. As it was, I did not choose to delve into this sort of research – perhaps worried that I might meet the ghost of Van Gennep in merely echoing his thesis of death as a passage and funeral rites as treating the deceased like an initiant who, after a period of separation and marginality, is reborn into a new life in the other world of the ancestors.

I think that my perception of the *bu'mpo* song did not really change until I began to pay closer attention to the text. I was surprised to notice that in each stanza personal names of a very particular sort were repeated – names that, I had been told, could only be pronounced in the secrecy of the enclosure where boys are initiated. Once I had noticed this repetition of forbidden names, I realized something I had previously overlooked: this repetition always occurred during this part of the ceremony.

Why did I now hear this song differently? Because in the meantime I had closely observed, during the course of boys' initiation (which lasted several months), a number of very long sequences one of which in particular, on the third day, involved giving each of the circumcised boys a secret name. The first among the circumcised – first to be led into the enclosure, first to be circumcised, and also first in that he was the chief or guardian of those undergoing initiation with him – received the name Yoamia. All the stanzas of the mourning song addressed this character, either as Yoamia or as 'master of the enclosure' (a title that during initiation was reserved for the chief circumcisor): 'Reveal to me the oracle, O circumcised one of the enclosure! Reveal to me, O Yoamia, reveal to me the oracular word!'

Now, if there was one secret that was, in principle, eternally kept from women, it was surely the secret of male initiation. Once I had identified the Yoamia character, I no longer had any doubt, after hearing the first stanza, about the question being put to the oracle. Through these voices, I realized, the women were publicly asking the men about their secret. Why, in this time of grief, were the women, who supposedly knew nothing about boys' initiation, trying to learn the secret from its first and chief keeper?

After decoding some of the words, I still had not found the key to this text. In other stanzas the two singers asked Yoamia questions about something that, at first, seemed paradoxical –

the secret of making millet cakes (a staple for the Gurmanceba). No one who has read Jaulin's (1967) book on initiation will be surprised to learn that my fieldwork turned up a whole series of equivalences between the way men 'made' new initiates and female procreation and food preparation. Although I shall not dwell on this, I would like to mention that, once I began to grasp the song's general meaning, the theoretical question raised by noticing that 'rites correspond to each other' seemed increasingly complicated.

Given the way this mourning song brought the theme of initiation into a funeral ceremony, I obviously could not be satisfied with an explanation that took it as a reminder of a critical date in the deceased's biography, the one marked by his circumcision ordeal. In fact, this explanation could be thrown out because this song was also performed at an old woman's funeral. At this point in my research I still felt that a musical metaphor was most appropriate for explaining how ritual made apparent contemporaries of characters who in fact belonged to different repertoires separated in time and space. It seemed to me that this sort of composition could best be explained in the terms used by musicologists when, in attempting to describe how different human or instrumental voices answer each other in certain fugues, they say that these voices 'enter in imitation'.

Having staked out a few reference marks – the identification of the forbidden names, the unexpected encounter with the theme of secrecy, and the metaphor of rites from two distinct ceremonies 'entering in imitation', I was thus led to modify my understanding of the space-time continuum of this segment of the funeral ceremony and also to re-examine certain rites within this ceremony that were of greater import than I had imagined. New questions arose that shed light on the scene enacted during the song. At first I had considered it a typical theatrical enactment of a transgression. Indeed, what was surprising about it was that women played the role of Yoamia. The words 'There is nothing, there is nothing in the initiation enclosure, there is nothing in the enclosure where we are sitting except women's screams of joy', sung by two women, were Yoamia's answer to the other women's questions. But this was not all.

As I have already said, the *bu'mpo* song was accompanied by a mime performed by the deceased's eldest daughter. What was it that she was miming? From her gestures one might say that it was both the acts about which the women were asking (e.g., the geomancer striking the sand as he interrogated the oracle) and Yoamia's answers. During this part of the ceremony the eldest daughter in fact took the place of the first among the circumcised. This was clearly confirmed when, at the end of the song, she abruptly stood and said to her brothers and sisters, 'Let's hurry – the chief circumciser is waiting for us'. In fact, Yoamia said the very same thing to his companions when they were reluctant to go to meet the chief circumciser at the entrance to the initiation enclosure. The way in which words and whole sentences reflected each other in the ritual led me to shift my observation post once again. In the midst of the funeral ceremony, the deceased's eldest daughter invited his offspring into the initiation enclosure. It seemed natural to me to take her invitation at face value.

One day, as I was listening to the boys singing in the initiation enclosure, I was amazed to notice that not only was their song similar to bu'mpo but also several couplets had identical words. The wounds of the initiates, who had been circumcised several weeks earlier, were now healed, and they had taken the ritual bath which marked a first stage in their transformation to the status of initiates. This transformation called for a change of regimen in the enclosure. They now had to learn more songs of a series they had begun learning on the first day. The song I had recognized was one of these new songs. Men and boys had, as they did every evening, taken their places facing each other in front of the enclosure, where the former would sing a couplet and the latter would repeat it.

The first part of this song had to do with the objects used during initiation that, because they immediately brought to mind the wounded genitals, were supposedly highly secret. These objects were all things in the circumcisor's kit: the razor blade, the hemostatic clips, the piece of bowed wood used to hold the wounded penis, cotton, the plants used for dressing wounds, etc. Each new couplet of the first part of the song mentioned one of these objects by name in a secret language. After its name was pronounced, a phrase reminded the initiates that it was not their initiators who were revealing the objects – that regardless of how ordinary they might be, such objects could be revealed only by the mythical ancestress who had invented the treatment for healing the wound of the first circumcised man.

It was the second part of this song that contained the couplets which were exactly the same as those of the *bu'mpo* song. This time, however, it was a previously circumcised one who was asking Yoamia – who was now in fact present – to reveal the oracular speech and, furthermore, following this first question with a series of other questions relating, as in the *bu'mpo* song, to the making of millet cakes. At the end of the song the reply to the questions came not from Yoamia but from a previously circumcised one: 'There is nothing in the enclosure where we are sitting except women's screams of joy'.

Had I heard right? I had to make sure by asking the instructors whether the words of the couplets they had just taught the initiates were really the same as those in *bu'mpo*. Their response more than reassured me of the accuracy of my hearing. Having anticipated that I would soon be asking about this sort of repetition, they provided me with explanations. At this stage, they said, the initiates were like orphans, without fathers or mothers. They did not know what was going to happen to them. They were uncertain about their 'new masters'. What was going to happen to them was like a secret that had to be extracted through geomancy from the earth's mouth. For this reason, the question put to the oracle was repeated in the song.

At the time that I received this explanation, I already knew that the ritual linked the transformation of the survivor's status following a parent's death to the 'metamorphosis' that adolescents underwent through initiation. I had been told several times that, during mourning, the deceased's compound was like the enclosure used for circumcision and the master of the mourning ceremonies (who would become the head of the household) like the 'master of the enclosure'. Furthermore, I had already sensed that the demonstration during the evening mourning session of certain inversion behaviours (living persons assuming the deceased's attributes and leaving their own attributes to the deceased, women playing male roles) was aimed at suggesting the idea of a time when the differences which enable us to recognize ourselves as living or dead, men or women, villagers or bush-dwellers are erased by the proximity of death. For me, a significant fact supporting this hypothesis was that one of the leading actors in the mourning ceremonies, the deceased's eldest daughter, played the role of Yoamia. By miming Yoamia, the eldest daughter was playing the role not of a man but of someone

whose sexual identity had not yet been fixed. If there was a time
in the ritual when all differences seemed to be suspended, it was
surely the time spent in the initiation enclosure.

Knowing or sensing as I did all this about the relationship
between mourning and initiation, what was it about hearing
bu'mpo in the initiation enclosure which could still surprise me?
I had first heard this song as a public interrogation of men by
women about the secret of the enclosure. I was now hearing an
interrogation formulated in the same terms and on the same
subject but this time by the previously circumcised in the very
place of the secret. In the light of the explanations which the
instructors of the novices had just provided, I felt that a question
had been posed by this song about the experience of loss in two
forms of initiation – the loss experienced by boys in the enclosure, at the very least their lost childhood, and the loss that,
through the funeral ceremony, created orphans, male or female,
mourning a parent. Beyond the obvious similarities (feeling of
abandonment, uncertainty about the future), the voices of the
previously circumcised during initiation and of the women during
mourning 'entered in imitation' and thus likened two types of
initiatory experience to each other: both orphans and initiates
experience a chill. The deceased's eldest daughter had led me
to a place where the question about the status of the orphan
became that of the loss experienced by the initiant. In this place,
too, however, the mourning song which the previously circumcised were singing taught me that the paradigmatic figure of
the orphan was being embodied by Yoamia, the first of the
circumcised.

The lines which led me from one ceremony to another can
now be described in the light of Wittgenstein's remarks. 'A
multiplicity of faces with common features continually reappearing here and there' – I know of no better metaphor for the effect
on me, at a particular stage of my study of Gurmanceba rites,
of the reiterated experience of an impression of similarity
between such-and-such a scene in the rite being conducted before
my eyes and the image summoned up by my memory of such-
and-such a fragment of another rite witnessed in the course
of previous observations of the same ethnic group. Was this a
straightforward case of evocation or an effect induced by the rite
itself, leading the observer to consider the similarity a reminder,
a (re)call in the present from an absent rite? I would perhaps

not have focused on this question had not my reiterated observation of a particular segment of the funerary rites induced in
me a need to trace the links between this ritual sequence and
another, as yet unknown but present among the many elements
that I had already registered in another rite. Of course, intellectual correlations can always be established between elements of
different rites on the basis of their similarity, but the observation
just mentioned provided me with criteria for recognizing the
procedure employed by the ritual to ensure that its perception
– by participants and observer alike – would induce in them the
reversal of an image which recalled another rite. The best idea
of this procedure is provided by the notion of a place change.
In the guise of a role change, a new space appears in which
actors occupy many places, and this is a perception which
immediately induces in the observing ethnologist a shift from
one rite to another that allows the recognition of one of the lines
it contains. It is this place change which, by doing away with the
apparent discontinuity of ritual life, enables that observer, so
long as he allows himself to be shifted by this movement, to give
'consistency' to the line he has identified on this occasion.

REFERENCES

Jaulin, R. (1967) *La mort sara: L'ordre de la vie, ou La pensée de la
mort au Tchad*, Paris: Plon, Terre Humaine.
Lévi-Strauss, C. (1971) *Mythologiques: L'homme nu*, Paris: Plon.
Smith, P. (1979) 'Aspects de l'organisation des rites', in M. Izard and
P. Smith (eds) *La fonction symbolique: Essai d'anthropologie*, Paris:
Gallimard.
Wittgenstein, L. (1982) 'Remarques sur le *Rameau d'or* de Frazer',
trans. J. Lacoste, in J. Bouveresse, *L'animal cérémoniel: Wittgenstein
et l'anthropologie*, Lausanne: l'Age d'Homme.

Chapter 3

Brothers and sisters in Brahmanic India

Charles Malamoud

The divinities of Vedic polytheism unarguably constitute a pantheon: in myth and above all in ritual, each god is distinguished from the others and co-ordinate with them; his personality is marked by the domain and modes of action assigned to him as well as by his physical and moral attributes. (The articulation between the various components of the divine world does not, of course, exclude rivalry or even hostility: the gods are frequently involved in conflict over the shares due to them in the various rites.) Nevertheless, these divine figures are often confused, and the features which give them shape are not enough to endow them with stable identities. Vedic theology strives on the one hand to undo the notion of a divine individual; being endowed with ubiquity, each god has several bodies or, rather, an infinite number of bodies, and his power can be decanted into the body of another god. The texts state continually that, considered from such-and-such an angle and in the particular circumstance created by the rite, one specific god is identical to such-and-such another one – that he quite simply *is* this other god. On the other hand, the kinship relations between the gods are the object of fragmentary and disparate statements. Some gods are known to be fathers or sons, and this genealogical positioning with reference to an ascendant or descendant, who is designated by name, may play a major role in their history and in the cult surrounding them. However, other divinities appear to have no family ties of any sort. Still others have the character of 'sons' even though it is impossible to tell who their fathers are; in fact, in the case of a god like Agni the question cannot even be phrased in these terms, for this god, above all else a son, is 'son of himself'.

Although the cosmogonic figure of Prajāpati undoubtedly came to dominate later Vedism and all the gods are derived from him as his sons, the same thing applies to all creatures and to all elements of the cosmos, human society, and ritual. This does not prevent this creator from being re-created in his turn, in both myth and rite, by his own creation; in this respect, the father is also the son of his sons (or, rather, of the particular son, the god Agni, who took the initiative in this re-creation). The scholars writing at the end of the Vedic period (in the *Bṛhaddevatā* and the *Nirukta*) were receptive to the notion of reciprocal and reversible filiation (*anyonyayonitā*) among these gods who give birth to each other (*itaretarajanmanaḥ*). Thus, the fact that we have trouble in distinguishing clearly the families of the gods is due not only to lacunae in the mythology but also to the desire of the Vedic theologians (who may have exploited these silent and obscure passages) to demonstrate that the identity of a god cannot be defined by the same criteria as are applied to the identity of a mortal. Furthermore, this blurring of their affiliation is repeated in a way with their alliances; some gods have one spouse, but in ritual there is the indistinct mass of the 'wives of the gods'. Kinship ties between gods may occasionally be stressed, but when this happens it is generally to reveal an instance of incest – Prajāpati's attempt to commit incest with his daughter Dawn (Uṣas) or Speech (Vāc) or the secret committing of incest with his daughter Saraṇyū of Tvaṣṭṛ 'the shaper'.

The brother-sister relationship among the gods is sometimes evoked; for instance, it is because Prajāpati desires their sister that the gods are scandalized by the passion which their common father feels for his daughter. However, the brother-sister relationship is represented above all by a famous couple, Yama and his twin sister Yamī. The two terms are common nouns, signifying 'twin boy' and 'twin girl', and it is clear that we are dealing here with a borderline case. Yama and Yamī are brother and sister par excellence. Everything said about them in the texts concerns both the nature of twins and the relationship between siblings of the opposite sex. Yama and Yamī are brother and sister and, moreover, twins; conversely, they are twins who are also boy and girl. There is, however, a very important difference between this brother and sister. The myth of Yamī comes down to the story of her relations with her brother; she exists only for, or at least with, him. Yama, in contrast, occupies his own place in the pantheon independent of Yamī: there are myths – accounts of the origins of rites – in which he appears without any reference to the one who makes him what his name says he is, a twin.

Apart from Yama and Yamī, the brother-sister relationship receives only rare and passing mention in the texts of ancient India, whether in religious or literary works or in that enormous mass of literature which is simultaneously one and the other. Brothers and sisters do of course feature among the hundreds of characters who appear in the Epics (and hence in the narratives or plays which are constructed on epic themes). There is, however, no trace of a paradigmatic situation in which the central issue is precisely this relationship. There is no evidence that ancient India provided a type for the brother of a sister or for the sister of a brother. One would search in vain through Indian traditions, at the very least the Sanskrit texts, for a sister who could be compared with Antigone or Elektra. This absence is all the more remarkable in that the theme of brothers (in Vedic mythology, Agni and his brothers; in the *Mahābhārata*, the five Pāṇḍava; in the *Rāmāyaṇa*, the figure of Rāma and his younger brother Lakṣmaṇa) is given very full treatment, as is the relationship between a man and his elder brother's wife (Lakṣmaṇa's fervent devotion to Sītā).

A case can be made, in classical Indian mythology, for the couple constituted by Kṛṣṇa and his sister Subhadrā, the wife of Arjuna, but here too it must be noted that the principal theme is the friendship between the two brothers-in-law; when the relationship between the brother and sister is put forward – notably in the Jagannāth procession – it gives the devotees an opportunity for joking about their incestuous intimacy. A very different type of example is provided by a relatively late literary text, the *Harṣacarita* of Bāṇa, a novel or, rather, romantic chronicle of the seventh century AD. In it the principal hero Harṣa converts to Buddhism; he has been led and preceded in his conversion by his young widowed sister, but, having taken the initiative by opening the way for her brother's spiritual transformation, she is told on asking to be admitted into holy orders, 'You must comply with your brother's orders because he is your elder, your *guru*, your brother, a man whom you love, your king'. It thus appears that the (elder) brother is very specifically the protector of a woman who no longer has a father or a husband.

Nevertheless, the prescriptive texts in Hinduism which define the status of women with the greatest authority are silent on the subject of brothers (see, e.g., the *Laws of Manu* (5. 147 ff.):

> A little girl, a young woman, a woman of advanced age, must never do anything according to her own will, even in her home. During her childhood, a woman must depend on her father, during her youth she depends on her husband; when her husband is dead, on her sons; a woman must never rule herself as she likes.

The commentary of Kullūka cites another collection of laws, that of Narada, and adds, 'if she has no son, she must depend on her husband's close relatives, and if there are none, on her father's close relatives. If she has no relative on either side, the king is considered her husband'. It is obvious that a woman's brothers are included among her father's close kin, but it is remarkable that no brother is expressly mentioned in the wording of this regulation.

Hindu practice, as observed nowadays, strikingly contrasts with the poverty and even the silence of the texts with respect to making the brother-sister relationship an essential element of ritual (although many clues also point to the fact that an ancient tradition is thereby being perpetuated). In short, the sister intervenes in a discrete but decisive and indispensable way in the rites which punctuate her brother's life. She ties around her brother real and symbolic bonds which provide his person with protective boundaries. Here are the principal data:

In northern India the feast of *rākhī-bandhan* is celebrated every year at full moon in the month of *śrāvan* (July–August), when a sister visits her brother to show him her affection and to tie a good-luck thread (*mangal-sūtra*) about his wrist. We have a developed version of this rite in Stevenson's description of the Gujrat Brahmans at the beginning of this century:

> On this day brothers invite their sisters to their homes, and, in return for the invitation, sisters send a thread to which they have tied a crushed areca-nut, thereby symbolically declaring that they have crushed and destroyed all their brother's troubles and worries.
>
> Arrived at her brother's house, the sister . . . places a low square stool and on that arranges three pipal leaves . . . on

the leaf to the right she arranges as many threads as she has
brothers . . . the brother gives presents to his sister: money,
cloth or bodice . . . after the meal the things are removed
from the stool and taken to the nearest pipal tree; there one
of the threads is tied to the tree, and the others are tied to
the wrist of the various brothers.

(Stevenson 1920: 304)

This rite has given rise to various interpretations which, while
they may be superimposed on it, must not be allowed to obscure
the elementary and fundamental fact that, by placing a 'protective thread' around a man's wrist, a woman is demonstrating that
this man is, to her, a brother; the same gesture may also signify
that a man and woman have become adoptive siblings, 'brother
and sister according to the *dharma*' (*dharm-bhāī/dharm-bahin*),
to each other, meaning that any possibility of marriage between
them is excluded and also that real familiarity is permitted
between them because intimacy cannot form a prelude to conju-
gal relations. As a barrier against incest, *rāhkī-bandhan* is also
the protective screen which makes tenderness innocuous (cf. Carstairs 1970: 71). Another notable feature is that, towards midday,
the brother gives his sister a meal, some money, and some
clothes. These are the presents typically given to the priest in
return for his ritual services. It may in turn be deduced that
when this form appears in the context of a ceremony, it is a sign
that the recipient of this gift has fulfilled functions of a sacerdotal
nature to the donor's benefit. It is a duty of this nature that the
sister is performing for and upon her brother. In fact, although
the brother and sister occupy symmetrical positions with reference to the marriage prohibition symbolized by the boundary
established by the thread, all the other elements of the ceremony
betray an asymmetry between the two partners: it is the sister
who, by means of a motion which she alone can perform,
executes a rite which is destined to bring her brother happiness
and produce visible and invisible effects for his benefit. What
the brother gives in exchange is not of the same order of things;
although the rite would certainly be incomplete and thus inoper-
ative if his sister's service were not remunerated, as far as she
is concerned the gifts she receives have no value other than their
intrinsic utility. This is precisely the asymmetry on which the
relationship between the sacrifier and the officiants is constructed

in Brahmanism (on the question of ritual honoraria, see Malamoud 1976).

When a boy who is a member of one of the three first 'classes' in Brahman society leaves his childhood behind him he receives an initiation (*upanayana*) which turns him into a 'twice-born' (*dvija*) – this second birth being conferred on him by Vedic words taught him by a master. He then enters a period of varying length of apprenticeship to the Veda. The initiation ceremony includes a 'sacrificial thread' (*yajñopavīta*) presented by the master to his pupil, which the twice-born will thenceforth constantly wear. (The manner of wearing it varies according to ritual circumstances; in everyday life and during worship of the gods the thread rests on his left shoulder, passing under his right arm; during funeral rites and ancestor worship, it rests on his right shoulder, passing under his left). Once he has put on the thread, the visible symbol of his second birth, the boy effectively belongs to his parents' caste and has acquired his full ritual personality. The Brahmanic texts provide ample data on the 'significance' of the thread, the number of fibres making it up, and the knots tied in it, but they do not specify the hand that has to spin it; similarly, and this silence is more surprising, they do not put forward any explanation for the fact that the sign of his second birth is a thread which permanently surrounds the initiate's torso (on this question, see Malamoud 1977: 135 ff). Light is shed on the first matter by some popular songs in northern India in the Bhojpuri dialect: from these we learn that the *janeu* (the form which the Sanskrit word *yajñopavīta* takes in vernacular Hindi) was not bought but spun in the home of the boy's sisters (Champion and Garcia 1989: 260). On the second point we need only observe that the thread forms a closed circle which does not in any way suggest a link between the one who wears it and any external anchorage, in the manner of the umbilical cord for instance, but rather is a loop or line which circumscribes the body born of this second birth.

The sister also intervenes in her brother's marriage rites. Here too we see her manipulating bonds, but this time it is to undo them – and not the thread binding part of her brother's body but the knot which binds the newly married couple together. After the ceremony proper has been celebrated in the bride's home, the couple goes to the bridegroom's. There, as Stevenson informs us (still in connection with the Gujrat Brahmans), the knot that tied the husband's scarf to his wife's sari is undone, and also the fruit that was bound on their wrists to guard them from the assaults of passion, the bride loosening that on her husband's wrist and vice versa. The sari and scarf, however, are untied by the husband's sister or aunt, who probably charges about five rupees for this service.

(Stevenson 1920: 103)

This is not so much a matter of carrying out a rite as of performing the motions which make it possible to get out of the rite. Nevertheless, these motions are themselves ritual, and it is the sister's sacerdotal function to undo the knot binding her brother to the wife he has just been given without actually undoing the very union which the knot symbolizes. Her brother (and his wife too, of course) regains the freedom of movement without which it would be impossible to lead a practical existence, but this material necessity is fulfilled in such a way as to enable him to enclose himself within his own contours.

We have seen that the duty of undoing the knot may also be performed by the bridegroom's aunt. The action takes place in the paternal home, and in this case it is the father's sister who is concerned. The same applies to the boy's other rites of passage, and in each case it is his paternal aunt who officiates, both in placing the thread and in tying the knot. Is she acting as a substitute for his sister? It seems more appropriate to consider her as sister to the boy's father. In other words, the sister enables her brother to fulfill his ritual obligations as father towards his son. If, as the texts encourage us to do, we apply the sacrificial scheme of things to the rites of passage, we observe that, in this case, the father assumes the role of sacrifier and that it is indeed for his benefit that his sister exercises her sacerdotal function by acting upon her nephew's person. Thus we see the paternal aunt of a newborn intervening in the name-giving rite (*nāmakaraṇa*): it is she who ensures that the name is chosen correctly and who ties the silken or cotton threads around the baby's wrists and ankles, around his middle, and to his cradle (Stevenson 1920: 13–14). The baby's first solid food (*annaprāśana*) consists of a mixture of milk, sugar, and rice which is placed on a gold or silver coin for him to lick. The coin is then given to his paternal aunt (Stevenson 1920: 19).

I must reiterate that our knowledge of the sister's role in the rites which structure her brother's life and, it seems to me, even his person are based only on observable practice. The canonic texts of Brahmanism, notably the *Kalpa-sūtra* (see Ram Gopal 1959; Kane 1930–62; Pandey 1969), provide abundant and precise instructions about the rites of passage (*saṃskāra*, lit. 'process of perfection'), but they do not contain any allusion to sisters. If, however, we go back to the very oldest Indian texts, the corpus of Vedic writings, we find formulas of hymns and prayers, outlines and summaries of myths, and sketches of poetic metaphors which enable us to build up a picture of a sister who, by the bonds which she offers or imposes on a man draws the boundaries which define his person, thereby rendering it continuous and coherent. The difference between the glimpses afforded by these texts and the information which we can deduce from the rites as they may nowadays be studied in the field is that in the latter case we are dealing with a sister who is in contact with her own brother, whereas in the case of the Veda we are in the presence of figures designated as 'the sister' of the gods or of the *ṛṣi* (the 'seers' to whom the Veda has been revealed).

Sisters and bonds: there is at least one passage in which this association is so close that it becomes a means of identification through the application of a metaphor. The poet evokes, sometimes by speaking of it and sometimes by talking to it, the grass belt which the master ties around his pupil, who is henceforth dedicated to study as well as to sexual continence:

> You are the arm of the seers, O belt . . . she was the daughter of Faith, born of ascetic fervour, *sister of the seers* who make the beings . . . this man [the pupil], with the mystery of the Vedic word, with the fervour of the ascetic, with the weariness of ritual work, *with this belt I sew him* . . .
>
> (*Atharva-saṃhitā* 6. 133. 3 ff., my emphasis).

After the sister of the seers, here now is a 'sister of the gods'. Her name is Rākā, and she is in some way the tutelary goddess or prototype of women who in the human world have the status of sister. She appears in a treatise on sacrifice, the *Aitareya-brāhmaṇa* (3.37), in which it is said that a particular phase of the *soma* offering requires the recitation of a series of stanzas (this textual whole forms the *Āgnimārutaśastra*) containing first a hymn glorifying the wives of the gods and only after these a hymn to Rākā; as the text tells us, the sister, although issued

from the same navel as her brother (she is *samanodaryā*), nevertheless passes after his wife, who is issued from a different navel
(*anyodaryā*), and lives in dependence on the wife. During the
sacrifice, the wife of the sacrifier stands back (that is, to the
west) from the fire, called Agni gārhapatya; it is, after all, the
god of fire who deposits sperm in wives' wombs. (Sisters, for
their part, are not admitted into their brothers' sacrificial pre-
cincts.) Nevertheless, the same text goes on to say that sisters
must also be honoured, reciting 2.32.4 of the *Ṛk-saṃhitā*, which
exalts Rākā, the sister of the gods:

> I invoke Rākā, whom it is good to invoke, with a fine song
> of praise. May she listen to us, the blessed one, may she notice
> it herself! May she sew her workpiece with a needle which
> does not break! May she give us [for a son] a hero worth a
> hundred such, a hero worthy of praise!

What is the work she is sewing? The *Brāhmaṇa* tells us: 'Rākā
it is who stitches the seam (*sevanī*) of the man, the seam which
is on his penis. Male sons are born to him who knows as much'.
The commentary of *Sāyaṇa* adds, 'It is the vein called *sira*; it
passes over the top of the penis and extends to the anus; the
goddess called Rākā firmly stitches this seam'. What this sister
divinity does to the sexual organs of mortal men gives us the
meaning of what human sisters do to the lives of their brothers
when they surround them with bonds; the sister is preventing
her brother from wasting himself and, notably, from wasting his
virile energy; she is giving him the corporeal or ritual sewing
which he needs to travel along the pathways of life (and to
disseminate his sperm only in the appropriate receptacles).

The pathways of life are first of all the paths of sacrifice: the
man sets out along them prepared and guided by his sister: 'For
you, Indra, the poet sets in motion this song of praise . . . which,
like a sister, leads your steps forward towards the sacrifice' (*Ṛk-
saṃhitā* 8.12.31, my emphasis). This mysterious stanza from the
Atharvaveda further gives us to understand that the sister's task
is to enlighten her brother about the itineraries of the rite
(*adhvara*): 'The mothers go along the paths [*adhvabhis*], they
who are the sisters of those who make the sacrifices [*jamayo
adhvarīyatām*]' (*Atharva-saṃhitā* 1.4.1).

We may note in passing that another sister of the gods, Silacī
or Arundhatī, is known to us on account of her talent for mend-

ing fractures and healing wounds. Mythology and medicine together present this divinity as the personification of a plant which 'climbs along trees'. 'The trails of resin [that she leaves] run along the bark like the creeper's tendrils, with which they may be compared' (Filliozat 1949: 110; Zysk 1985: 75, 98, 202–3). In this case, too, a sister is seen to be working with bonds and bindings.

For the sister, sewing her brother and turning him into a 'nicely trussed-up' being, protected and strengthened by the boundaries which define him, involves above all designating the boundary of incest and marking the fact that, however close she is to her brother and however embracing she may be, she herself lies beyond this boundary. She officiates for her brother: the fact is that she cannot be a wife to him. In Vedic Sanskrit, one of the common terms for sister is *jāmi*, which, in its substantive form and fixed in its feminine mode, is the adjective which really means 'consanguineal'. The *jāmi* is a being who cannot be a *mithuna*, a 'sexual partner'. (This term can also assume the meaning of 'paired couple'; see Renou 1958a: 46–50; 1958b: 47–8). Thus when two *jāmi* unite or attempt to unite, they become guilty of incest. It is remarkable that the supreme *jāmi* should be the sister. This is not to say that copulating with a mother or daughter would be any less serious a matter. On the contrary, it seems that these transgressions among humans are so abominable that it is better not even to think about them. (For a list of women with whom a man may not copulate under pain of committing incest, see *Viṣṇu-smṛti* 34.1). What the texts do most readily talk about is the act which at once constitutes the paramount example of incest and the most horrible sin, although it concerns a symbolic relationship: coupling with the wife of one's spiritual master (see *Manu* 11.171). The inference is that a man is constantly subjected to the temptation to unite with his sister, which renders it necessary to turn the very word 'sister' into a permanent reminder of the prohibition. Through the Veda we know of at least one text, albeit a fairly obscure one, which evokes in the manner of a denial the act of love (*kāmyam*) between *jāmi*, brother and sister, as a burning gentleness (*priyaṃ dagdham*). There seems to be an analogy to two sticks rubbed together to produce a flame; by uniting, *jāmi* commit the prohibited *ajāmi*, which is improper for blood kin.

Jāmitva, 'consanguinity', conceived above all as risk of incest, is, by extension, characteristic of redundancy, superfluity, and bad repetition of the same thing. In this meaning the term *jām-itva*, accompanied by its antonym *ajāmitva*, is very frequently employed in Vedic treatises on sacrifice: an excessive similarity between two acts or two consecutive statements or between two adjacent ritual objects is a fault – a fault of excess, so to speak, and condemnable for the same reasons and in the same terms as incest (see *Mīmāmsā-kosa*, s.v. *jāmi*). At each stage of the rite there appear elements which must be combined into *mithuna*, pairings; only on this condition does the sacrifice yield results. It is therefore desirable to avoid associations of identical or excessively similar objects or words. Whenever this is required, care is taken to introduce one or more differences, 'in view of the *ajāmitva*, for non-redundancy, in view of the *mithunatva*, the [correct and fecund] pairing.' Thus, in a rite which involves the simultaneous consecration of water, which in such circumstances is said to represent 'all the divinities', and of ghee, 'the corporeal form of all the gods', one must be careful not to pronounce a prose formula (*yajus*) for each but to murmur this prose formula for the clarified butter and to recite loudly a poetic rhythmic formula (*chandas*), possibly a stanza of the *Rgveda*, for the water (*Taittirīya-brāhmana* 3.3, 4, 6). These endlessly reiterated pre-scriptions take on meaning only if one recognizes the sexual characteristics conferred on the various elements of the rite at very least by the grammatical genders of the names they bear. These prescriptions also assume, although it only became explicit in a later period, among the ritualistic philosopherss of the *Mīmāmsā*, that one determines the sequences in which repetition is proscribed just as, in the domain of kinship, one circumscribes the network within which union constitutes incest. However strong the wish to avoid redundancy, the necessarily repetitive character of the rite cannot be annulled. Finally, the need to repeat the prohibition of repetition does not itself come under the same ban: these constantly reiterated formulas are part of the discourse on the rite and not of the rite itself.

Attempted, narrowly avoided, or secretly committed incest – this is the uncertainty around which Indian myth about the origin of mortal men revolves. It is found in its most developed form in hymn 10.10 of the *Rgveda*; a dialogue builds up between Yama and his twin sister Yamī, consisting of fourteen alternating stanzas, with the odd stanzas spoken by Yamī and the even ones by Yama. Thus Yamī takes the initiative, proposing to her brother in increasingly pressing and passionate terms that he make love with her, for the sake of pleasure but also for that of procreation. In fact, her ardent desire is that Yama should found a race. She knows that the race of mortal men must be born of Yama, who is a god but who – following some unknown event – has become the first mortal and at the same time the ruler and judge of the kingdom of the dead (and thus the prototype of the king). His achievement is to have found the paths which lead to that other world in which the dead are to experience a form of survival, having been transformed into ancestors by the funeral rites which their survivors celebrate for them. In order to set up this system and people this kingdom, however, the first mortal must unite with a partner who is homogeneous with him: Yama must unite with Yamī. Yamī's argument runs thus: 'That is what the immortals want: descendants for the sole mortal. Let your mind bend to ours. Penetrate as husband the body of your wife' (stanza 3). 'Love for Yama has overwhelmed Yamī', she says farther on. 'I want to lie with him on the same couch. Like a wife with her husband, I want to deliver my body to him. Let us roll it, let us shake it, as the two wheels roll and shake a chariot' (stanza 7).

Yama, however, turns away. Each of his replies is a refusal. He does not want to see Yamī's passion as anything more than the ardent impulses of a girl who has become nubile and needs a man. When Yamī invokes the will of the immortals, Yama reminds her of another law, the one forbidding two *jāmi*, two beings who share the same origin, the 'same navel', from coupling. Such is the supreme institution, the *dhāman*, watched over by two other gods, Mitra and Varuṇa, whom nothing eludes.

The poem ends with their melancholy agreement; Yamī resigns herself and, while reproaching Yama for his weakness, predicts that another woman will embrace him. Yama repeats her words along with an injunction worth noting: 'You will embrace another man, Yamī, and another, indeed, will embrace you . . . make a happy marriage'.

Humanity nevertheless exists. The race of mortals worships the race of the dead and recognizes in Yama the figure of the first to have been capable of passing through death. Yama founded the human condition and rules over humans both here and in the world beyond. Is he also their ancestor? We do not know. Yama and Yamī separated before they had accomplished the act which would have given birth to the human race. No other narrative takes up the story: humanity is the fruit of an act of incest which either never took place or has disappeared without a trace.

In the course of the discussion Yamī presents an unexpected and very far-reaching argument – that while they are indeed *jāmi* to each other, their twin nature, far from strengthening the bond of consanguinity which links them as might be thought, erases the boundary between them. They issue from the same womb, but in this womb they lay side by side, a sign, according to Yamī, that they were destined to lie together once they had been born (stanza 5). What is more, there is a famous example of two *jāmi* who are associated as a *mithuna* couple; they are Sky and Earth, about whom we learn in another hymn (3.54.7) that they are 'two young sisters' who are nevertheless called by names which designate them as sexual partners. Likewise in 1.159.4, Sky and Earth are two divine parents 'two sisters of the same womb [*jamī sayonī*], of the same habitat [*samokasa*]' and *mithuna* to each other (see Renou 1965: 89, 92; 1966: 92). In the language of the hymns, in fact, the name of Earth is always and the name of Sky very often female.

What we are seeing here is a reversal which, while it certainly has no effect on real life or on legality, can be observed in vocabulary and myths: the culmination of the sibling state is twins of the same sex. When this extreme point has been attained, the definition of a sibling as one with whom it is impossible to form a couple is abolished; the constellation of Gemini bears the name *mithuna*, and in the Vedic pantheon the male twins (possibly also riders) called Aśvin are, if not designated *mithuna*, at least closely associated with this notion of fecund coupling:

> The gods did not know where to find prosperity. They saw it in the act of fecund coupling. But they were not able to agree on the subject. The Aśvin said: 'It is ours. Do not come to reclaim it from us'. Thus it belonged solely to the Aśvin. Any man who wants to achieve prosperity must immolate a twin cow destined for the Aśvin. He is thus resorting to the Aśvin by offering them the share that properly belongs to them.
>
> (*Taittirīya-saṃhitā* 2.1, 9, 4)

With Yama and Yamī, twins of opposite sex, we are half-way

there; Yama insists that they are brother and sister and therefore may not copulate, while Yamī stresses that they are twins and have been predisposed to *mithuna* since their intra-uterine life together.

In the human world there is a feast called Yama-dvitīya (the second [day] of Yama) or Bhrātṛ-dvitīya (the second [day] of the brothers, in Hindi Bhāī-bījā), under the sign of Yama and Yamī, on the second day of the clear fortnight in the month of Kārttika (October–November). This feast is attested as early as the *Purāṇa* and in the work of Bhoja (eleventh century) and still flourishes today in northern India. (Its very name exemplifies the importance attributed to the notion of 'two' and of 'second' in everything connected with Yama. This twin god is marked by his duality; already in the Veda, the kingdom of the dead over which he rules is guarded by two dogs who have two pairs of eyes each, and in post-Vedic mythology he is given a very complicated genealogy of twins and doubles [Malamoud 1980: 95ff].) In the case of a brother, this feast involves paying a visit to his married sister, who receives him in private and shows him marks of honour and tenderness: she bathes him, massages him, and gives him food. The rite involves the enactment of a mythological scene; Yamī, in the form of the River Yamunā, welcomes her brother Yama, who has been able to leave the kingdom of the dead for a day. What is more, he has given his subjects the day off; if they have sisters to house them, the dead are given permission to come and spend this day among the living (and custom, it is said, dictates that prisoners enjoy a few hours of freedom on that day). Neither the sister's husband nor her children play any role in this event. It is indeed a meeting between brother and sister, alone as Yama and Yamī were, although Yama and Yamī are evoked in a manner which recalls their tenderness, the attempted *mithuna* summoned by their twin nature, and not Yama's virtuous refusal of his sister Yamī.

Consequently, this feast is quite the opposite of the rites of passage which mark the brother's life-cycle and require specifically sacerdotal services from the sister. This ceremony commemorates an unreal act of incest, with no prohibition and no fecundity. On that day, in regions bordering on the Yamunā River, brothers bathe in those sisterly waters; thus they mingle their bodies with the bodies of their sisters, or at least with the body of the one who was the supreme twin sister, beside whom they dream that they slept beneath their mother's navel before they awoke to be born.

REFERENCES

Carstairs, G. M. (1970) *The Twice-Born: A Study of a Community of High-Caste Hindus*, London: Hogarth Press.

Champion, C., and Garcia, R. (1989) *Littérature orale villageoise de l'Inde du Nord*, Paris: Editions de l'Ecole Française d'Extrême-Orient.

Filliozat, J. (1949) *La doctrine classique de la médecine indienne: Ses origines et ses parallèles grecs*, Paris: Imprimerie Nationale.

Kane, P. V. (1930–62) *History of Dharmaśāstra (Ancient and Medieval Religious and Civil Law in India)*, 5 vols., Poona: Government Oriental Series.

Malamoud, C. (1976) 'Terminer le sacrifice: remarques sur les honoraires rituels dans le brahmanisme', in M. Biardeau and C. Malamoud, *Le sacrifice dans l'Inde ancienne*, Paris: Presses Universitaires de France.

——— (1977) *Le svādhyāya, récitation personnelle du Veda: Taittirīya-Āraṇyaka, livre II*, Paris: E. de Boccard.

——— (1980) 'La dualité, la mort, la loi: note sur le nombre deux dans la pensée de l'Inde brahmanique', *Revue d'Esthétique*, nos. 1/2.

Pandey, R. B. (1969) *Hindu Saṃskāras: Socio-religious Study of the Hindu Sacraments*, 2nd edn, Delhi, Varanasi, and Patna: Motilal Banarsi Das.

Ram Gopal (1959) *India of Vedic Kalpasūtras*, Delhi: National Publishing House.

Renou, L. (1958a) *Etudes sur le vocabulaire du Ṛgveda*, Pondicherry: Institut Français d'Indologie.

——— (1958b) *Etudes védiques et pāṇinéennes*, vol. 4, Paris: E. de Boccard.

——— (1965) *Etudes védiques et pāṇinéennes*, vol. 14, Paris: E. de Boccard.

——— (1966) *Etudes védiques et pāṇinéennes*, vol. 15, Paris: E. de Boccard.

Stevenson, S. (1920) *The Rites of the Twice-Born*, London: Oxford University Press.

Zysk, K. G. (1985) *Religious Healing in the Veda*, Transactions of the American Philosophical Society, 75, 7.

Chapter 4

The brother–married-sister relationship and marriage ceremonies as sacrificial rites: a case study from northern India

Raymond Jamous

Anthropological analyses of rites can be divided into three types on the basis of their theoretical and methodological approaches. One of these has paid particular attention to the psychological[1] and social[2] functions of rites, while a second has classified rites according to their purposes.[3] These two approaches are combined when rites are considered as means of serving purposes beyond themselves; the ritual action in which a series of representations is manifested is not studied in terms of its own logic but considered as the expression of other logics (psychological, economic, etc.). A third approach, centred on certain rites or collections of rites, has subordinated their functional character to the search for a classification which would reveal their mechanisms – the arrangements and processes they develop for effecting transformation. The works of Hertz (1960) on funerary rites, Van Gennep (1960 [1909]) on rites of passage, and Hubert and Mauss (1964 [1898]) on sacrifice express the various tendencies which mark this approach. Hertz studies the treatment of different components of death, especially the task of mourning during second funerals in one particular region, South-East Asia. He introduces a comparison between these rites and representations of death in other societies. Van Gennep is more ambitious: on the one hand, he extracts from the corpus of life-cycle rituals three main stages, processes, or sequences (rites of separation, of the margin, and of reaggregation) through which the main ritual actor passes in order to change his status, rank, or social position; on the other hand, he shows how rites of passage serve as models for understanding other rites (agricultural rites, warrior rites, etc.). Some have questioned the importance and the degree of elaboration of various 'preliminary', 'liminary', and 'postliminary' rites in the ceremonies studied here. One might wonder, as Mauss (1968: 553–5) has, whether Van Gennep was too hasty in generalizing his propositions, thus emptying his concept of 'passage' of any precise content. However, the problems inherent in his analysis do not detract from the fact that he has posed an important question: Do all the rites in a given society have similar mechanisms? Do they have the same weight, or are some so important that they inflect the forms assumed by the others? Hubert and Mauss's analysis of sacrifice seems at first sight to fall half-way between Hertz's approach and Van Gennep's. They have exposed the mechanisms common to sacrificial rites in all their diversity: on the one hand, the distinctions between sacrificer, sacrifier, victim, and divinity and the way in which they are related through the mediation of consecration, immolation, and sharing of the victim and rites of liberation. Sacrifice thus becomes a 'procedure [which] consists in establishing a means of communication between the sacred and the profane worlds through the mediation of a victim, that is, of a thing that in the course of the ceremony is destroyed' (Hubert and Mauss 1964 [1898]: 97). Although Hubert and Mauss do not attempt to apply their model to other types of rites, their analysis nevertheless enabled Durkheim to clarify his distinction between the sacred and the profane and to define his general perspective for the study of Australian religions and rites.

In the variants of this third approach, ritual mechanisms[4] are not only those which set words and gestures, objects and subjects, or ritual actors in relation to each other but also and especially those which manifest the transformation of relations between the different social actors, living or dead, spirits or gods. The distinction between the three stages of rites of passage underlines this movement, as does the idea of 'communication' and 'establishing contact' between profane and sacred worlds through sacrifice.[5]

Van Gennep's analysis differs fundamentally from that of Hubert and Mauss: in rites of passage, the accent is on the principal actor, whether initiate, bridegroom, deceased, or mourner, the other actors enabling or attending his transformation; in the case of sacrifice, the asymmetrical relations between sacrifiers and sacrificers, victims and divinities are the objects of ritual transformations as the various ceremonies unfold by a specialized process of identification and differentiation. This is a matter not

of choosing among analytical perspectives but simply of understanding the implications of each.

It is striking to observe that these various questions raised by
anthropology have been addressed by the Vedic literature of
India. As Lévi (1898) and Renou (1978), followed by Malamoud
(1989), have demonstrated, the Indian thinkers of the Vedic
period were constantly holding forth upon rites. The latter were
considered from a general point of view as characterizing man's
activity and the construction of the cosmos. They were also
classified notably as solemn or domestic. It was, however, more
from the point of view of sacrifice than of rites of passage that
their mechanisms were examined. Malamoud has stressed the
fact that sacrifice appears in these interpretations both as a particular rite and as a model for other rites. Although sacrifice is
no longer the dominant rite in the concrete Indian societies
studied by anthropologists, the hypothesis formulated here is
that its mechanisms are still at work. I will show that marriage
ceremonies among the Meo of northern India, while indeed constituting a rite of passage, are founded primarily on the ritual
principles of sacrifice.

The Meo live in the Mewat area (situated in the middle of a
triangle drawn between Delhi, Jaipur, and Agra) and make up
nearly a quarter of its population (250,000 persons of a total
population of more than 1,000,000). They are a Muslim community and locally claim the status of Rajput, a high warrior
caste. They live in villages alongside other castes, most of which
are Hindu, and generally occupy the position of dominant caste,
having pre-eminent rights to the agricultural land. In order to
place the description outlined in the following pages, one must
begin by understanding (1) that the Meo engage in an asymmetrical form of marriage alliance – isogamic in type – between large
exogamous patrilineal groups,[6] each unit always receiving women
from the same groups without ever giving women in return and
giving women to other groups without ever receiving them in
return; (2) that a man may not marry within his clan, his village,
or his mother's village; (3) that a man may reproduce his paternal
grandfather's or his paternal uncle's marriage but not his father's;
and (4) that the rites of marriage, like Hindu rites in the region,[7]
are primarily the affair of the two families forming the alliance,
only secondarily that of their respective patrilineages, and never
that of the large groups involved in the marriage alliance.

MARRIAGE CEREMONIES

In every union we must distinguish among the preparatory rites, the wedding, and its ritual extensions.

Preparatory rites

The preparatory rites are conducted simultaneously but separately in the house and village on each side of the marriage. They are similiar for the bride and the bridegroom; we will follow their course in the case of the latter.

Emissaries are sent to various houses in the village and other villages to summon relatives and friends to the wedding. This invitation is called the *nota* and constitutes a ceremony in itself: the emissary does not simply relay the invitation but gives a small sum of money (between a penny and tenpence) to the invited person, who commits himself on accepting it to attend the ceremonies.

The father of the bridegroom seeks out his various married sisters, taking them gifts. One of them, generally the eldest, will become the *sahvasani*, the principal officiant in the bridegroom's preparatory rites. Under these circumstances, the position she holds in relation to her brother and his children is equivalent to that held by a priest of the Brahman caste in relation to castes inferior to himself, notably the warrior castes. She is assisted by a barber, and both the bridegroom's mother and his sisters are under her authority. She officiates during the rites of the bath (*batnā*) and the procession to the forest (*banvarā*),[8] which consecrate the bridegroom and elevate him to royal dignity. In return for all these ritual services she receives *neg*, ritual honoraria in money or in kind.

The *batnā* consists of bathing with mustard oil (*tel*) sent by the bride's parents. In this task the *sahvāsanī* is assisted by the barber and the *bhābī*, generally the wife of the bridegroom's eldest brother. After bathing in water, the bridegroom stands on a plank (*patra*) while the barber massages his body with mustard oil: first his hands and arms (beginning on the right), then his face, his shoulders, his chest, and his back, and finally his lower limbs. The young man puts on new clothes, and the *sahvāsanī* ties a yellow cord (*kangnā*) around his right wrist and places a crown with hanging threads that cover his face (*sehrā*) on his head. Then she performs *arti* before the threshold of the house, rotating around the bridegroom's head a copper tray on which are placed a lighted candle, one or two *paisa* (farthings), some rice, a herb called *dub*, and a copper pitcher (*lota*) half-filled with water.

After his bath, the bridegroom, wearing the *sehra* and carrying an iron cane (*butā*), both royal insignia, goes in a procession called the *banvarā* 'to the forest', which begins symbolically at the boundary of the village residential area. He is flanked by two young companions who guide him and accompanied by the *sahvāsanī* and the barber, who carries the tray. They are followed by singing *bahin*, 'sisters' of the bridegroom. As the procession passes the houses of the quarter, their inhabitants come forward and place one or two *paisa* in the pitcher after having rotated them around the bridegroom's head. At the boundary of the residential area, the *sahvāsanī* once again performs *arti*. The procession returns to the bridegroom's house and then repeats the ritual. Once the *banvarā* has been accomplished, the bridegroom removes his crown and his new clothes and goes to bed.

The *batnā* and the *banvarā* are repeated several days in succession. After the first *batnā* and *banvarā*, the bridegroom has to observe certain rules (and the same applies to the bride). He may no longer leave the village residential area on his own without risking attack by *bhūt*, wandering malignant spirits which could possess him, drive him mad, or even kill him. If he does go out to the fields, he must be accompanied by a friend of his own age. He must keep close at hand the cane or sword (*talvar*) that is the attribute of his royal status and protects him against malignant spirits. He must stop working. He is forbidden to lie on the knotted rope bed (*carpaī*) and must sleep on the ground. He must abstain from eating meat and peppered and bitter foodstuffs; he may eat only vegetable food cooked with a little butter and sweetened.

The *batnā* and the *banvarā* constitute rites of separation and consecration. Prior to them, the bride and bridegroom are not distinguished from others. After them, they are, in their respective villages, elevated above their ordinary condition as a king and queen are. This transformation is a consecration and places the future spouses in a state of purity which renders them fragile while at the same time ensuring them protection, through the prohibitions, against the dangers represented by evil spirits.

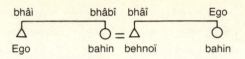

bhâi   bhâbî bhâî   Ego

Ego   bahin behnoï   bahin

Figure 1 Metasibling relations

On the eve of the marriage feast, after at least the first baths and processions, the bridegroom's maternal uncle, accompanied by some of his agnatic kin, comes to offer *bhāt* (lit. 'boiled rice') – a collection of presents of cloth, jewels, and money – to his sister and her husband, the latter's sister (who officiates at the preparatory rites), and his nephew, the bridegroom. His brother-in-law welcomes him at the village boundary and accompanies him to the men's part of the house (*bangla*) while his wife is getting ready for the ceremony. Traditionally, the sister would wait on the threshold of their home with a copper pitcher on her head, her husband behind her holding a copper tray containing rice and *dub*. Her brother would put some money in the pitcher, salute her, and place the *bhāt* on the tray. He would then produce a rupee for each house of the lineage and a rupee for each member of the *panchayat* (the village assembly). Once he had made these prestations, he would be invited with all his agnatic kin into the house, where he would be given a meal. Nowadays the pitcher is no longer used, and the sister carries the tray and receives the gifts, with her husband simply standing behind her.

In short, the consecration of each of the future spouses demands complementary ritual action by two persons: the paternal aunt (*phûphî*), who receives in return for her ritual services honoraria from the bridegroom's father, and the maternal uncle (*māmā*), whose ceremonial prestation 'nourishes' his sister's family as well as the *sahvāsanī* and somehow acknowledges the latter's ritual labours. Thus the ceremonial roles are distributed between a pair of relatives, the paternal aunt and the maternal uncle. In fact the paternal aunt is above all the father's sister (his *bahin*) and the maternal uncle the mother's brother (her *bhâî*); inversely, the bridegroom is above all the brother's son in the case of a female ego and the sister's son in the case of a male ego. The central relationships are those between two brother-sister pairs linked by a marriage (Figure 1). I use the term 'metasiblingship' for this specific form of brother-sister relationship, which transcends the distinction between blood and

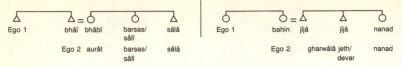

Figure 2 Sibling and affinal relations

affinal kin. In fact, this metasiblingship is expressed in two ways: on the level of ego's generation, where the terms *bhâî* 'brother' and *bahin* 'sister' are used to designate all members whatever their origin, and in the narrower context in which the use of *bhâî* and *bahin* characterizes the chain of brother-sister relationships that I call opposite-sex metasiblingship. In this chain, a male ego designates as *bahin* not only his sister but also the sister of his sister's husband, and, reciprocally, a female ego considers *bhâî* not only her brother but also the brother of her brother's wife. This chain contrasts with that composed of same-sex siblings, who are distinguished from their immediate affinal relatives by specific terms: a male ego differentiates between his brother (*bhâî*) and the brother of his brother's wife (*sâlâ*); a female ego differentiates between her sister (*bahin*) and the sister of her sister's husband (*nanad*) (Figure 2).

The terms *bhâî* and *bahin* vary in meaning according to which chain they occur in. In the one case they express relations of metasiblingship and in the other relations of consanguinity. Within this terminology, marriage assumes two meanings: one as the expression of metasiblingship the other as a manifestation of affinity. While the preparatory rites of marriage activate the chain of opposite-sex metasiblingship those of the wedding itself involve making distinctions between blood and affinal relatives.

The wedding

The last ceremonial moment to take place on both sides of the marriage is a prestation known as *nota* by various agnatic relatives and other consanguineal *bhâî*. This gift of money, the amount of which is entered in an exercise book, establishes a debt relationship between blood relatives and must be paid back in the course of another ceremony.

The wedding takes place in the bride's village. The bridegroom dresses himself in his new clothes and crown and takes the cane just as he did after his first bath; he is king. Accompanied by a group called *barat*, made up of a number of his agnatic relatives, he goes to his future wife's home. The *barat*'s stay lasts between one and three days and is punctuated by a series of prestations from the bride's to the bridegroom's side (the prestations going in the other direction are minor and are directed primarily to the bride), the most important of which are the 'gift' of the bride (*kanyā-dān*) and the 'gift' of the dowry (*dān-dahej*). These involve specialized gifts from the bride's father to the bridegroom (from father-in-law [*susar*] to son-in-law [*asnaw*]). The asymmetrical relationship of affinity which is marked by these prestations establishes a hierarchical superiority of recipient to donor. As Parry (1986) has observed, the *dān* is a gift that is not reciprocated.[9] The gift of the bride must be that of a virgin, purified and adorned with all her jewels. The 'given' bride is not an object any more than the cow offered to the Brahman is only an animal; she possesses a sacred quality and in a certain sense a divine spark.[10] This gift to the bridegroom is equivalent to the gift made to the Brahman (Dumont 1980: 117) and places him in a position superior to that of the donor.[11]

Can it be said that this gift of the bride has the effect of transferring her wholly from her group of origin to that of her husband? The *dān* does not merely involve the transfer of property and valuable goods[12] but constitutes the setting for the relationship between the two partners rather than, as some have thought, the substance that establishes it. It remains associated with the donor as much as the recipient; in particular, the young wife will remain affiliated with her group of origin while being integrated into her husband's family. The 'given' bride does not cease to be a sister; indeed (and this is an essential point) *she remains the sister (bahin) by the very fact of her marriage*. The bride as *kanyā-dān* is not a prestation like the others: she is not only an object given, passing between the male partners, but also subsequently an acting subject, a principal officiant in the life-cycle rites of her brother's family.

The bride has put on her new clothes after a final bath and is getting ready to leave. She is weeping and has to be pushed into the car to join her husband there. Her maternal uncle gives her a few rupees before her departure, and her paternal aunt does not allow the car to leave the village until she has received a small sum of money from the couple. When they arrive in the boy's village, it is his paternal aunt and not his mother who receives them in front of their future home. She performs *arti* for them, receives a *neg*, and then allows them to enter.

After a brief stay with her husband, the bride returns to her parents for an unspecified period. A final ceremony with specialized prestations leads to the bride's definitive installation in her husband's village and concludes their marriage rites. However, although these rites are over, their effects continue to be manifested long afterwards.

Extensions of the marriage ceremonies

In the following generation, at the birth of children to a couple which has been constituted in this manner (particularly in the case of its first son), at the circumcisions of their male children, and at the marriages of their children of either sex, we rediscover the feature which characterized the beginning of the marriage rites as described above: ritual services by the married sister and ceremonial prestations by the brother.

A woman who has been given in marriage has to return to officiate for her brother and bring additional life to her family. First of all, at the birth of his children, in particular the first son, she comes to perform an important purification ritual for mother and infant.[13] On the third day after the lying-in, she washes her sister-in-law's breasts and draws her first milk. The couple gives the sister a *neg*. The role of the married sister is not so much that of removing impurity as of establishing the mother-infant relationship in the domain of purity; her first ritual intervention in her brother's home is complementary to the action the mother takes for her baby's survival.[14] Circumcision rites are similar to the ones for marriage. In both cases, the married sister plays the role of *sahvāsanī*: she is the principal ritual officiant, assisted by the barber, and receives ritual payment (*neg*) from her brother for her services. In these various rites, this married sister succeeds the paternal aunt who officiated at her brother's marriage. Her ceremonial role will in turn cease after the marriage of her brother's children.

The woman's brother, for his part, brings to his brother-in-law (*behnoi*)'s village a collection of gifts (cloths, money) called *cucak* at the birth of his first son,[15] *bhāt* at the boys' circumcisions, and *bhāt* again at the marriages of all the couple's children. His prestations end with this generation. At first sight,

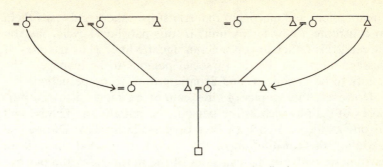

Figure 3 Metasiblingship relations in diachrony

these prestations seem to extend the links of affinity established at his sister's marriage, but there are two major differences: it is the wife's brother who brings the gifts and not her father (or one of his representatives), and it is the sister (the one who was given away with the dowry) who has become the recipient: she receives the gifts with her husband. Although the prestations of the father to his daughter's husband have now been taken on by the brother, the latter is in fact assuming the same ritual role as that of his own maternal uncle. In so doing he takes his place, along with the married sister of the children's father, in a new chain of opposite-sex metasiblingship. The ritual extensions of the wedding pertain not to affinal kinship but to metasiblingship in the form of a new chain of two brother-sister pairs linked by a marriage. In this they are similar to the preceding generation's preparatory rites to a marriage (Figure 3).[16]

MARRIAGE CEREMONIES AS RITES OF PASSAGE AND AS SACRIFICE

Marriage and rites of passage

Meo marriage ceremonies are rites of passage. In fact, the principal actors, the bride and the bridegroom, pass through three stages: separation from their celibate states through the mediation of preparatory rites (baths and processions), a period of marginality or liminality during which they may not work and are subjected to very strict prohibitions, and, finally, reintegration into the community in their new social statuses as husband and wife. Their children pursue a ritual trajectory (birth, circumcision, and marriage) that transforms them and leads them to constitute a new family unit. In this patrilineal cycle, the son succeeds his father to continue an agnatic line. Thus the rites of passage allow the destiny of social persons to be managed, the family to be organized, and agnatic groups to be perpetuated.

However, this corpus of rites cannot be reduced to the purposes of entities such as the person, the initiate, the family, and so on, as the reference to rites of passage implies. During the wedding, the constitution of the couple is effected through an asymmetry between the two sides of the marriage by the passage of a woman as a gift, the latter being the sign and not the cause of the recipient's superiority over the donor. What is more, being married entails responsibilities not only in the home; a man has obligations towards his married sister and her children, and his wife for her part must officiate at rites in her brother's home. This indicates that no household or family withdraws within itself or defines itself according to its own criteria. As in the caste system, interdependence is the basic feature of the Meo kinship system. The mother's brother and the father's married sister are at least as essential to their nephews and nieces as their parents.

In short, the couple is constituted through affinal ties between the two sides of the marriage. It becomes an indivisible unit, a family, only when the wife's brother and the husband's married sister are attached to it and when it is inserted into the series of brother–married sister relationships that I have called the chain of opposite-sex metasiblingship. The couple or family is not an autonomous unit but is closely associated with a double series of relationships, those of affinity and those of metasiblingship.

Marriage and sacrifice

Comparison with Brahmanic interpretations of sacrifice may be helpful in clarifying my theme. My intention here is not to establish correspondences feature for feature or to reduce marriage rites to sacrifice. If sacrifice constitutes the model for rites in India, it is not in terms of an earlier norm which persists in variously degraded forms but in terms of a structure the mechanisms and ritual principles of which are still operative. From this point of view, the comparison must respect the specificity and coherence of Meo marriage rites and sacrifice so as to identify similarities only on the level of the structural properties of each whole. The hypothesis is that behind the variation lies a cultural unity of Indian civilization expressed in its rites. For the purposes of this comparison, I rely basically on the works of Malamoud, who, following Lévi and Hubert and Mauss, has extended and renewed the consideration of sacrifice on a number of points.

To start with, I want to stress the analogy between Meo marriage rites and those which are the object of interpretations in Sanskrit texts. Malamoud notes that, in classical India,

> the marriage ceremony can be viewed as either *saṃskāra* or *yajña*. As *saṃskāra* (perfecting), marriage is one event among others in the sacramental life of each spouse. It is a rite of passage that places the young man in a position to establish his hearth, to become *grhastha* [master of the house]. For both the man and the woman, this ceremony is a *dīksā*, a consecration preparatory to that enduring sacrificial session that is the couple's life. As *yana* (sacrifice), marriage has to do not only with the biography of each spouse but also with that of the group formed primarily by the young man, the young woman, the young woman's father, and the *purohita* [priests] of the two families.
>
> (Malamoud 1974–5: 123–4, my translation)[17]

In this context, the girl's father is the sacrifier, she is the victim, and her husband is both the divinity who receives the offering and the sacrificial priest. Malamoud thus encourages us not to take the sacrifice literally. Immolation, properly speaking, is not part of this Vedic interpretation of marriage. The girl is offered as victim but becomes wife; the boy plays the role of divinity and sacrificer but becomes her spouse. A couple established in this way will have its own sacrificial fire and henceforth be able to play the role of sacrifier.

The Meo wedding stresses affinal ties: asymmetry between the donor, the girl's father, and the recipient, the husband, implies the passage of a 'consecrated' victim, the girl considered a gift. This homology also suggests that the gift is similar to a sacrificial offering or, to paraphrase Malamoud, becomes significant within the logic of sacrifice (Malamoud 1976).

Meo marriage rites involving metasiblingship may also be characterized as a manifestation of sacrifice. The preparatory rites of marriage are analogous to the *dīksā* (consecration) of the person offering the sacrifice, during which he must 'divest himself of his profane body and invest himself with a sacrificial body' (Malamoud 1989: 80, my translation).[18] In Meo marriage ceremonies, the married sister consecrates her nephew, who 'dies' to his celibate status to be 'reborn' during the wedding as a king before becoming head of a household. The married sister officiates in a sense as a 'sacrificer' for her brother and his son, who constitute the group of 'sacrifiers', and she receives honoraria analogous to the *dakṣiṇā* paid to the sacrificer. A rite of passage (with a 'death' and a 'rebirth') is thus inflected by its fundamental relationship to the mechanism of sacrifice.[19]

Marriage, sacrifice, and temporality

The first comparison, which reveals the element of sacrifice in the play of asymmetrical relationships in Meo rituals, must now be supplemented by one which takes into account the diachronic aspect of the rites.

As Malamoud observes,

> at first sight the rites form linear series of acts which have a beginning (and an end). There is a moment when one leaves profane life to enter into the rite and a moment when one leaves the rite to return to profane life or to enter into another rite. [For the Brahman writers, however,] the beginning is a redoubtable threshold, a violent opening; it is advisable to invent symbolisms, to discover points of view which reduce the strangeness of the moment of beginning and rob it of its impact . . . Certainly a rite begins. However, this beginning is made up of or preceded by (we do not know which) a series of preliminaries, preludes, preparations, introductions during which the rite gradually assumes its form but in which the beginning as such is fragmented and diluted.
>
> (Malamoud 1987–8: 121, my translation)[20]

The solemn sacrifice is preceded by a consecration, this being the *dīksā*, which is itself preceded by the declaration of intent to perform a sacrifice, the invitation by the sacrifier, the offering presented, etc.

> The idea of beginning is the more blurred in that, in some respects, the preliminary *dīksā* is in the final analysis the essence of the sacrifice. [A Vedic text stresses,] 'Its beginning

is its end, and its end is also its beginning'. The text draws its argument from a feature of the rite's structure, to wit, that the concluding oblation . . . is modelled on the introductory oblation to state that the beginning and the end of the sacrifice merge . . . This text . . . asserts fairly clearly . . . the wish to tack onto the effective experience of linearity and irreversibility of the sacrificial sequence caught between a beginning and an end the symbolism of never-beginning/always-beginning-anew.

(Malamoud 1987–8: 122, my translation)[21]

I consider these diachronic properties of sacrifice to apply to Meo marriage rites. Here again, the problem is knowing when the marriage ceremonies begin – when the guests are invited? when the married sister arrives? when the bride and bridegroom are being prepared? What is more, these important preparatory rites are not real beginnings; they refer to previous marriages of which they are the conclusions. Thus one may go back indefinitely without finding any notion of an absolute beginning. In the chain of Meo ritual sequences, one starts by activating the chains of opposite-sex metasiblingship, the consequence and conclusion of preceding marriages, which open the way for the affirmation of affinal ties which in their turn entail the establishment of new relationships of opposite-sex metasiblingship, and so on. In this diachrony, the chains of metasiblingship constitute the central aspect of the rites: a niece succeeds her paternal aunt, a nephew his maternal uncle. Conversely, the affinal ties between the two families are but momentary, because there can be no union between these families in the following generation.

Among the Meo, even during the ritual moments when affinal ties are in the foreground, opposite-sex metasiblingship continues to be manifested, to make its mark, and to frame the ceremonies. During the whole of the wedding, the bride and bridegroom are dressed as they were at their first consecration bath; the bride's paternal aunt continues to operate (she greets the eldest member of the *barat* at the door of the house and receives the gifts meant for the bride); at the moment of departure the maternal uncle must give them a small sum of money and the paternal aunt receive a ritual payment; in the bridegroom's village, it is his paternal aunt who welcomes the couple and performs the rites of entry into their new house. Although the prestations made in the course of the wedding basically involve relationships between men, the sisters, the bride's paternal aunts, must pour scorn on the *barat* as if to remind them that it is the given woman and not her husband who will occupy a pre-eminent place in her home village and will return to officiate in her brother's house.

The *kanyā-dān*, the gift of the bride, does not simply transfer a woman as a 'sacrificial offering' to some affinal kin but transforms a sister, who by marrying is not merely a given object but will become an active subject, an officiant, in her place of birth. I will venture to address this important point by drawing an analogy with the notion of remainders in Indian thinking about sacrifice. Here too, I refer to Malamoud (1989: 32, my translation)[22]: 'until they are incorporated into the hierarchical process of the sacrifice, food left-overs are objects of repulsion; when they appear as the remnants of a *yajña* they become supremely edible food and play an essential role in the continuity of the *dharma*. In this context, no victim or offering is eaten or consumed entirely; 'a remainder is left which, while ambiguous, has the permanent characteristic of being not inert but active'. Returning to the Meo case, it can be observed that giving a daughter does not mean losing her. Although she certainly is transferred to her husband's group, she remains linked to her family; more precisely, she is a remainder, the transformed married sister who will henceforth be active in her group of origin and bring it additional life.

The foregoing analysis leads to two important comments:

1. We must somehow decentre any view we may have of marriage ceremonies. The essential phases of the ceremony are the preparatory phases of the marriage and the consecration of the sacrifier, his *dīksā*.

2. There is no univocal principle which is automatically passed down from generation to generation but a complementarity of a hierarchical order between a predominant principle, the brother- –married sister relationship, and a subordinate one, the relationship between fathers-in-law and sons-in-law or, again, the relationship between brothers-in-law. The repetition (of meta-siblingship) cannot be realized without this detour into what is discontinuous and different (affinity); in the same way, it can only be reaffirmed through the mediation of the other.

Marriage, sacrifice, and the 'profane' world

Finally, sacrifice has one further property which in my opinion applies to marriage ceremonies, and that is the consequences or the effectiveness of the rite. Malamoud further stresses that the effects of the sacrifice do not cease when the rite ends; rather, 'an *apûrva* (unprecedented) force . . . makes the effects of the act ripen, even though the latter has run out' (1989: 67, my translation).[23] The sacrificial act not only influences the next sacrifice but also has effects on profane life. Malamoud's conclusion is that

> the distance between the sacrificial gesture and its consequence prevents and renders useless any feedback; thus sacrifice is an autonomous mechanism, a closed system; the actions which constitute it are outlines of actions and therefore at once differ radically from the actions of profane existence, with their failures, their ambiguities, and their changes of meaning even as they are being carried out, and serve as a model for those actions.
>
> (Malamoud 1989: 67, my translation)[24]

In the Meo community, an unmarried sister is not distinguished from her brothers by being the object of any particular attention. From the moment she is given away – once she has become the sister that her marriage has made her – her brothers' behaviour towards her changes; they must delegate one among them, the eldest, to make ceremonial prestations during rites involving her children and to ask her to officiate at rites involving her nephews and nieces. Her marriage produces effects beyond the moment of union with her husband. This, however, is not all. In everyday life, whenever a married sister pays her brother a visit she is treated with great respect both by her unmarried sisters and her sisters-in-law and by her brothers; her words are listened to, and her decisions have to be carried out. When she returns home, each of her brothers has to present her with a sum of money. The same applies when a brother pays his married sister a visit; he is obliged to make various prestations, as on the occasion of the *bhāt*, to her (and her husband), to her children, to her husband's sister, to her husband's parents, and so on. All these gifts and behaviours reproduce ritual actions. In other words, the everyday world must, without merging with the rite, be marked by it and model itself on it. Far from being functional in the sense of the effect of an external cause, the rite itself defines the frame of its significance and has consequences for everyday life.

RITES OF PASSAGE AND SACRIFICE

Stressing an interpretation in terms of rites of passage means not only analysing the ritual mechanisms but also associating them with purposes beyond the rites themselves. The purpose of the processes of separation, marginality, and reintegration is to transform the personal or collective statuses of the central actors. Once the rite has ended, the acquired status functions according to criteria which are not necessarily those of rites of passage. This is a context in which ritual and everyday or profane worlds are, in spite of their interdependence, derived from different and complementary principles. In this case, it is essential to mark clearly the beginning and the end of the rites.

In the case of sacrifice, in contrast, personal or collective purpose is subordinated to the ritual work proper. Ritual mechanisms serve nothing but themselves, at least not in any central way. They create a world of relationships and activate and transform it. Within this context, the problem is not how to separate rite from non-rite, profane from sacred, but how to link the rites in terms of the passage of time and of repetition. It is clear that in this context rites can have no beginning and no absolute origin.

In this analysis of Meo marriage ceremonies, we have not had to choose between these two interpretations; both have been shown to be valid. It is clear, however, that the rite of passage is subsumed by the sacrifice and the purposes of subjects by the world of relationships.

NOTES

1 The function of the ritual is to calm the anxiety that arises from confrontation with the unforeseen, the unknown, the incommensurable, the event that eludes understanding and technical action, and the uncontrolled, which is the source of chaos and disorder (Otto 1958) or renders practical action hazardous (Malinowski 1931). It is a way of meeting this external danger not on the practical or scientific

but on the psychological level. It allows a person to be reassured or to take courage and go forward again with tenfold strength.

2 Integration (Durkheim 1957; Radcliffe-Brown 1939), communion (Robertson-Smith 1927), communication (Leach 1966), or, inversely, a domination which reflects a kind of non-recognition (Bourdieu 1977).

3 There are many such classifications, but the one that has dominated the literature is the distinction between religious and magical rites (see Otto 1958; Durkheim 1957; Malinowski 1931).

4 According to Van Gennep, these mechanisms are more formal in nature, whereas according to Hubert and Mauss they closely link actions and representations.

5 This analysis of sacrifice is well known to have had an important effect on Hocart's (1970) construction of the notion of 'identification' or 'equivalence', the ambiguity of which still raises problems.

6 These lineages are segments of clans which are themselves endo-gamous. The ancestors of these clans are said to have been born of Hindu gods.

7 Only one marriage ceremony, the *nikah* or 'contract', is Muslim.

8 This term can be translated literally as 'he who goes to the forest'. It does not distinguish between cultivated fields and the forest proper.

9 Parry (1986: 453–73) insists on the analogy between gift and sacrifice: 'as the victim is a surrogate for the sacrifier so the gift is a surrogate for the donor' (p. 461). I will return to this aspect of things later on.

10 The bride leaving for her husband's home is adorned like the statues of goddesses that are carried in processions. The Meo consider her a queen, analogous to these mythological personages of divine essence.

11 Gray (1980) claims that the *kanyā-dān* is a sort of divine and pure gift on which the asymmetry between the two sides to the marriage is founded. It is difficult to accept this search for a substance to explain this relationship, as if it were sufficient to say that it is the gift of a cow which renders the Brahman superior; one could just as well say the opposite, that the divine gift renders the donor superior. Indeed, the problem lies in his wish to make the substance the essential thing, whereas the gift and the asymmetrical relationship go together without any need to look for cause-and-effect connections.

12 Parry makes no specific reference to the *kanyā-dān*. He indicates that on the general level the gift is neither a loan nor a wage and adds, 'It is alienated in an absolute way, and the very definition of the gift is that it involves the complete extinction of the donor's *proprietary* rights in favour of the recipient' (Parry 1986: 461). He reduces the question of the gift to a legal problem, a transfer of property rights. In my opinion, this singularly reduces the significance of this type of prestation and raises the problem of the notion of property, here understood as private property.

13 The lying-in and the ensuing period are marked by the impurity of mother and infant. The mother has to lie on a wooden plank so as

not to touch the ground. The attendant midwife comes from a lowly caste. The amniotic fluid must flow onto ashes, and the whole lot must be buried in the jungle. The placenta is buried beneath the house entrance if the baby is a boy and at the far end of a room if it is a girl. The umbilical cord is wrapped in a cloth and, like the foreskin, placed beneath the thatched roof. The mother remains in bed for three days and avoids touching the ground so as not to sully the house; she keeps her birth-polluted clothes on. The child is cleaned and wrapped in a cloth by the midwife and for three days is given only water mixed with cane sugar (*gur*) to drink. (*Gur* is distributed to children especially before the start of important rites and is considered to have a favourable effect on the ceremonial proceedings. Moreover, one of the last rites of marriage is that in which a little boy comes and sits on the new couple's laps and says, 'A child for you and some *gur* for me'. Thus to feed a child *gur* is to place his future under favourable auspices.) On the third day, mother and infant bathe and put on new clothes; the old ones are destroyed or given to untouchables.

14 This rite is called *chuchi dhona* and described in the case of the village of Shanti Nagar by Freed and Freed (1980: 369), who interpret it as a protection rite for the child after the period of pollution which he has undergone at his birth.

15 The maternal uncle brings his gifts only after the principal rites (in order, those of the purifying bath, the first breastfeeding, the attribution of a name, and the first haircut) are over. Similar data may be found in the description of Shanti Nagar by Freed and Freed (1980: esp. 399–401).

16 My intention is not to compare these Meo rites with those of neighbouring groups in northern India, but I must comment on the numerous analogies between the rites of this Muslim community and those of neighbouring Hindu groups. There are striking similarities in the way ceremonies are conducted, the order of sequences, the system of prestations and counter-prestations, the asymmetry between recipient and donor, and the ritual role of the maternal uncle, who must provide the *cucak* and the *bhāt* for the ceremonies involving his sister's children. Regarding the ritual role of the paternal aunt, the data are still fragmentary and do not allow systematic comparison, but the many clues – notably in Meerut and in Shanti Nagar (a village on the outskirts of Delhi) – seem to indicate that married sisters occupy a pre-eminent position in their group of origin, where they intervene in the rites of the ages of life. Having said this, I must point out that the Muslim Meos have no Brahman as priest, which gives greater weight to the married sister's ritual function. In my opinion, this difference does not fundamentally alter the manner in which kinship, in these northern Indian groups, is deployed in the rites. In the preparatory phases of marriage, the complementarity between the ceremonial prestations by the bride's brother and the ritual services of the father's married sister is central; during the wedding, the asymmetry between the two sides of the marriage

enables the couple to be constituted, and, as a consequence of the marriage rites, new chains of brother–married sister relationships are ritually manifested.

17 'En tant que *saṃskāra* (perfectionnement), le mariage est un événement – parmi d'autres de la vie sacramentelle de chacun des deux époux. C'est un rite de passage qui met le jeune homme en état d'installer son feu, de devenir *grhastha*. Pour l'homme comme pour la femme, cette cérémonie est une *dīksā*, consécration préparatoire à cette session sacrificielle de longue durée . . . qu'est la vie du couple. En tant que sacrifice, *yajña*, le mariage concerne non plus seulement la biographie propre de chacun des deux époux mais encore le groupe formé principalement par le jeune homme, la jeune fille, le père de la jeune fille, et les *purohita* de chacune des deux familles'.

18 'se dépouiller de son corps profane et se donner un corps sacrificiel'.

19 In the course of the marriage, which is considered a sacrifice in the Brahmanic sense of the term, the same person assumes different ritual positions in accordance with moments in the ceremony; the bridegroom, during the preparatory phases, is a sort of 'sacrifier'; during the wedding he occupies a place equivalent to the 'sacrificer', receiving a gift, and he becomes a sacrifier by assuming his new role as master of the house. This transformation touches the young woman; after having been a sacrifier as his future wife, she is offered up as a victim in order then to assist her sacrifier husband and to become the sacrificer, the principal officiant, in her brother's house. However, while the same persons hold different ritual roles according to their situations, the fundamental asymmetrical relationship of sacrificer-sacrifier remains operative throughout.

20 'les rites forment des séries linéaires d'actes qui ont un commencement (et une fin). Il y a un moment où l'on sort de la vie profane pour entrer dans le rite, il y a un moment où on quitte le rite pour retourner à la vie profane, ou pour entrer dans un autre rite. [Cependant pour les auteurs brahmaniques,] le commencement est un seuil redoutable, une entame violente: il convient d'inventer des symbolismes, de découvrir des points de vue qui font sortir de sa singularité le moment du début et lui font perdre son tranchant . . . Certes un rite commence. Mais ce commencement est fait, ou précédé, on ne sait, d'une série de préliminaires, préludes, préparatifs, introductions pendant lesquels le rite prend peu à peu consistance mais dans lesquels le commencement en tant que tel se fragmente et se dilue'.

21 'L'idée de commencement est d'autant mieux brouillée qu'à certains égards c'est la *dīksā* préliminaire qui est en fin de compte l'essentiel du sacrifice lui-même. [Un texte védique souligne:] 'its beginning is its end, and its end is also its beginning'. Le texte tire argument d'un trait de la structure du rite, à savoir que l'oblation conclusive . . . se modèle sur l'oblation introductive pour affirmer que le début et la fin du sacrifice se confondent . . . Ce texte . . . dit assez clairement . . . la volonté de plaquer sur l'expérience effective

de la linéarité et de l'irréversibilité de la séquence sacrificielle prise entre un début et une fin le symbolisme du jamais-commencé-toujours-recommencé'. Malamoud also notes that 'this desire [in his statements concerning the prose of ancient India] not to make what presents itself as the beginning into an absolute origin and, in short, this rejection of the idea of beginning go well with the structure of Vedic cosmogonies: origin is repetition, and before and after are inverted' (p. 121: 'Cette volonté de ne pas faire de ce qui se présente comme le commencement une origine absolue et en somme ce refus de l'idée de commencement s'accordent avec la structure des cosmogonies védiques: l'origine est répétition, et l'avant et l'après s'intervertissent').

22 'Tant qu'ils ne sont pas insérés dans les processus hiérarchiques du sacrifice, les reliefs d'aliments sont l'objet de répulsion; quand ils apparaissent comme les restes d'un *yajña*, ils deviennent nourriture comestible par excellence et jouent un rôle essentiel dans la continuité du *dharma*. [Dans ce contexte, aucune victime, aucune offrande n'est consumée dans sa totalité;] un reste demeure, ambigu, mais qui a pour caractéristique permanente d'être non pas inerte mais actif'.

23 'une force *apûrva* [sans précédent] . . . fera mûrir des effets de l'acte, alors même qui celui-ci sera épuisé'.

24 'La distance entre le geste sacrificiel et sa conséquence interdit et rend inutile tout feed-back: par là même, le sacrifice est une machinerie autonome, un système clos; les actes qui le constituent sont des épures d'actes: par quoi ils sont à la fois radicalement différents des actes de la vie profane, avec leurs ratés, leurs ambiguïtés, leurs changements de sens au cours même de leur exécution; par quoi ils servent de modèle aux actes de la vie profane'.

REFERENCES

Bourdieu, P. (1977) *Outline of a Theory of Practice*, Cambridge: Cambridge University Press.

Dumont, L. (1980) *Homo Hierarchicus: The Caste System and Its Implications*, rev. edn, Chicago: University of Chicago Press.

Durkheim, E. (1957 [1915]) *The Elementary Forms of the Religious Life*, trans. J. W. Swain, London: Allen and Unwin.

Freed, R., and Freed, S. (1980) *Rites of Passage in Shanti Nagar*, New York: American Museum of Natural History.

Gray, J. (1980) 'Hypergamy, kinship, and caste among the Chetris of Nepal', *Contributions to Indian Sociology*, 14: 1–33.

Hertz, R. (1960) *Death and the Right Hand*, trans. R. Needham and C. Needham, Aberdeen: Cohen and West.

Hocart, A. M. (1970) *Kings and Councillors*, Chicago: University of Chicago Press.

Hubert, H., and Mauss, M. (1964 [1898]) *Sacrifice: Its Nature and Function*, trans. W. D. Halls, Chicago: University of Chicago Press.

Leach, E. (1966) 'Ritualization in man in relation to conceptual and social development', *Philosophical Transactions of the Royal Society of London* B, no. 772, 251: 403–8.

Lévi, S. (1898) *La doctrine du sacrifice dans les Brâhmanas*, Paris: Leroux.

Malamoud, C. (1974–5) 'Résumé des conférences et travaux', *Annuaire de l'EPHE, 5th section*.

——(1976) 'Terminer le sacrifice: remarques sur les honoraires rituels dans le brahmanisme', in M. Biardeau and C. Malamoud (eds) *Le sacrifice dans l'Inde ancienne*, Paris: Presses Universitaires de France.

——(1987–8) 'Résumé des conférences et travaux', *Annuaire de l'EPHE, 5th section*.

——(1989) *Cuire le monde: Rites et pensées dans l'Inde ancienne*, Paris: La Découverte.

Malinowski, B. (1931) 'Culture', in *Encyclopedia of the Social Services*, Vol IV.

Mauss, M. (1968 [1950]) *Sociologie et Anthropologie*, Paris: P.V.F.

Otto, R. (1958) *The Idea of the Holy: An Inquiry into the Non-rational Factor in the Idea of the Divine and Its Relation to the Rational*, Oxford: Oxford University Press.

Parry, J. (1986) 'The gift, the Indian gift, and the "Indian gift"', *Man*, n.s., 21: 443–73.

Radcliffe-Brown, A. R. (1939) *Taboo*, Cambridge: Cambridge University Press.

Renou, L. (1978) *L'Inde fondamentale*, Paris: Hermann.

Robertson-Smith, W. (1927 [1889]) *Lectures on the Religion of the Semites*, 3rd edn, London: Macmillan.

Van Gennep, A. (1960 [1909]) *The Rites of Passage*, trans. M. B. Vizedom and G. L. Caffe, Chicago: University of Chicago Press.

Chapter 5

Transforming Tobelo ritual

J. D. M. Platenkamp

> *A village means not being alone,*
> *knowing that in the people, the plants,*
> *and the earth there is something of yourself.*
> Cesare Pavese, *La luna e i falò*

It is becoming increasingly evident that the hierarchical order of relationships which constitutes the social morphology of various eastern Indonesian societies is revealed above all in rituals. Recent comparative analysis of rituals from various societies has revealed that the meaning and value of these relationships are articulated in the transfer of beings and things and that such transfers, viewed in their totality, constitute systems of circulation (Barraud and Platenkamp 1990; cf. Barraud *et al.* 1984). Analyses of this kind generally concern rituals which are part of the indigenous traditions of the societies in question. In spite of the fact that most eastern Indonesian societies have been converted or are in the process of being converted to Islam or Christianity, little is known about the impact of such conversions on the rituals in which these circulations are effectuated. This analysis of ritual acts performed by the Tobelo[1] in a Christian church setting serves to explore this complex issue.

The Tobelo are a non-Austronesian-speaking people of the eastern part of the northern peninsula of Halmahera and the island of Morotai in the northern Moluccas. Each year at the end of the month of April, when the Christian inhabitants of the village of Paca have finished harvesting the rice, married women offer plates of locally produced rice and items of basketry for sale in the village church during a series of Sunday services. All the households in the village are expected to contribute goods, and each of them is expected to purchase at least one item. Refusal to comply would inflict 'shame'. Later, women from neighbouring villages are invited to participate in these auctions, and this is reciprocated when on future occasions village women offer their goods for sale in the neighbouring village churches. Although these goods are sold auction-style, it is understood that the rice at least should fetch a higher price than the imported rice sold in the local shops. There are other features to indicate that these auctions are not ordinary market transactions. The households whose goods are sold are not entitled to the money; it becomes part of the 'church funds' (Indonesian *kas gereja*), to be spent for a variety of public purposes, notably for the money prestations made at the marriages of church members' sons. Since, moreover, each household offers the same type of goods as it buys, judged from a purely market point of view the transaction is superfluous. The obligatory nature of the collective participation, the peculiarity of the exchange, and its very church setting indicate that what is involved is a ritual rather than an economic transaction.

Some eight months later, on the first Sunday of January, church prayers are said for the dead. Afterwards, each household decorates the graves of its deceased with flowers, whereupon the women, some dressed in military garments, parade through the village and, assuming provocative behaviour, enter houses to claim fruit and sweets.

Apart from being associated with the village church, these two series of events do not at first glance seem to be connected. The timing, for instance, of the auctions is determined by the rice harvest and that of the parade by the New Year according to the Gregorian calendar. A comparison with pre-Christian rituals, however, reveals that similar acts used to be part of a consecutive series of rituals in which both transfers of rice and money and parades of women in military garments figured prominently. The question here is whether these ritual acts, nowadays performed on separate occasions, are transformations of the acts which constituted the pre-Christian ritual cycle and consequently should be understood in relation to the pre-Christian rituals – such as the marriage ritual – which are still performed in Tobelo society to this day.

THE DEAD AND THE GENESIS OF SOCIETY

Tobelo villages, comprising between 300 and 1,400 inhabitants, consist of households of nuclear families (Indonesian *rumah tangga*) grouped in larger, ideally patrilineal units called 'trunks' (*utu*; Moluccan Malay *fam*). Trunks are related in two ways. First, there are relationships connecting a 'trunk on the man's side' (*o utu o naur-ino*) to several 'trunks on the woman's side' (*o utu o ngoheka-ino*). From the perspective of one's own trunk, the trunk of one's mother's brother, that of one's sister's children, and that of one's daughter's children are all trunks on the woman's side. This type of intertrunk relationship therefore gives a diachronic cast to affinity, connecting trunks over the generations through the women received and given in marriage. Repetitive marriage alliances between trunks are prohibited. Intertrunk relationships of this kind are explicitly modelled on processes of vegetable reproduction and multiplication. The bride is represented as a 'fruit' 'picked' from her native 'trunk' to be 'planted' in her husband's 'yard'. The second type of intertrunk relationship is that connecting separate trunks to constitute 'the people of one House' (*o tau moi ma nyawa*). Such trunks relate to one another as 'elder/younger (*ria-dodoto* 'elder/younger same-sex siblings') trunks on the man's side'. Whereas affinity generates relationships between trunks on the man's side and trunks on the woman's side, in the next generation these relationships are transformed into relations between elder and younger trunks on the man's side. In diachronic perspective, affinally related trunks can be incorporated in the course of three generations into the overall structure of the House. This incorporation entails that the trunks in question acknowledge – through their participation in certain rituals – as their 'originator' (*dodadi*, from *ho dadi* 'to come into existence') the same founding ancestor. These originators were the first to acquire title to the water and the land of a particular territory (*hoana*) 'for the benefit of their children and grandchildren'.

Social relationships are thus embedded in cosmological relationships, and in this respect a particular ideologeme (Dumont 1977: 35) *ma dutu*, is of fundamental importance. This construct designates a hierarchical relationship between two or more terms. The superior term represents the 'owner' (*ma dutu*) of inferior terms; the latter are 'owned by' and 'belong to' the former. All intertrunk relationships are classified as *ma dutu* (true, own), whereas non-kin relations are called *ma homoa* (strange, from elsewhere). It is through affinity that *ma homoa* relations are transformed in due time into *ma dutu* relations. The relations maintained with the founding ancestors who own the water and the land are also called *ma dutu*, and so are those which connect plants and animals with spiritual owners. All *ma dutu* relationships are ultimately subordinated to an all-encompassing concept of 'ownership' which is referred to as *jou ma dutu* (lord owner). Nowadays, Christian Tobelo address God by this term.

The ontological values attached to *ma dutu* relationships are articulated in myths of the Tobelo and other North Halmaheran societies (Platenkamp 1988b). These myths stipulate that the genesis of the first human beings is preceded by the construction of the *ma dutu* relationships which connect these humans to the spiritual owners of their constituent parts. These parts are labelled *roëhe* (body) and *gurumini*. Located in the person's blood and liver, *gurumini* is associated with his individuation as indicated by his personal name, his bodily shape (delineated, for instance, in his shadow), and his facial characteristics. For reasons elaborated elsewhere (Platenkamp 1988a: 14–17) I translate *gurumini* as 'image'. The fundamental idea prevails that the 'life' of all beings and things (*gikiri* 'being alive' as indicated by a stirring movement) is generated by the conjunction of image and matter.

A myth from the closely related Galela tells how the bodies of the first man and woman were formed from earth. To use the soil in a certain area for this purpose, an unspecified spiritual 'owner of the land' (*o tonaka ma dutu*) had to be removed from that area to be replaced by specified owners of that particular plot. These spiritual owners are a male and a female of a certain animal species; their bodies are made of decaying matter (*in casu* 'faeces') taken from the body of the original owner of the land, and they lack image. In this latter respect they are incomplete. An anonymous emissary of the all-encompassing lord owner inserts image into the human bodies formed from the soil and thereby renders them living, thus establishing the relationship between body and image which constitutes life.[2] This relationship enables the first man and woman to reproduce, and the woman gives birth to a son. The river that borders the plot where the woman has begun to cultivate rice begins to flood and destroys half of her garden; she curses the water and subsequently bears a second son who has only a 'half-body'. On the command of the lord owner, this second son submerges himself in a heavenly source of water in which a 'complete image' is reflected, to reappear as a 'whole' human being. The first son, although already 'complete as he is', voluntarily also submerges himself in the heavenly water, to re-emerge with the particular animal image reflected in this water. This makes him the owner of the descendants of the second son. A second mediating position is thereby created, viz., that between the lord owner, associated with heavenly water, and all of the younger brother's future descendants (cf. Platenkamp 1988a: 23–5).

The spiritual animal couple that mediates between the owner of the land and the first human beings is identified in terms of having bodies made of decaying matter. This is also the way in which the first stage into which each human being enters after death is identified. This stage is marked by the decay of the body and by the temporary expulsion, immediately after death, of his image from village society. The second mediating position, that of a single male identified in terms of a specific animal image, is linked with the second stage, in which the deceased exists as an ancestral image, which, once the decay of the body has been completed, is ritually reincorporated into society and may live on embodied in a particular animal species (Platenkamp 1988a: 97–110). Such ancestral images are associated as 'owners of the water' (*o akere ma dutu*) with the lakes or the rivers that mark the territories of the various Tobelo villages. The myth thus stipulates that in order to establish the relationship between image and body which constitutes life, the dead, both as decaying bodies and as bodyless images, must pre-exist. In the absence of the dead-as-decaying-bodies, man's body disintegrates at the very moment it is created, whereas in the absence of the dead as images, both the rice garden and the younger son are reduced to 'incompleteness'. However, the absence of ancestral image does not affect the first-born son. Both the primal creation of a man and a woman and the subsequent reproduction of a single son result from the conjunction of bodily matter, controlled by the specified dead-as-decaying-bodies, with an image that still derives from the universal heavenly source represented by the notion of the lord owner. As long as this is the case one son can be complete, but the multiplication of both rice and children cannot be accomplished. It is this multiplication, rather than mere reproduction, which requires that the image of the founding ancestor of a particular society be identified. In the light of the rituals to be discussed presently, it is highly significant that, in the sequence of events outlined in the myth, the initial absence of identified ancestral images affects the multiplication of rice, instead of the multiplication of people, first.

THE PRE-CHRISTIAN FIRST MORTUARY RITUAL

The death of a person is conceived of as resulting from a disjunction between his body and his image. This necessitates the expulsion of his image from the society of the living. This is not a 'natural' phenomenon but one that must be accomplished by ritual. One of the first acts performed after someone has died is a shaman's conducting the deceased's image to domains beyond village society.[3] These domains are controlled by the so-called *moroka*, *widadari*, or *jini*. As beings 'who already lived here long ago', these are manifestations of the autochthonous people who lived in the region prior to the Tobelo and who have since 'lost their smell of decay' and their visibility. Residing in the forest, the skies, and the deep sea, they are not part of village society. Accordingly, they lack identifiable images.[4] The image of the deceased is placed in their domains 'to lose its smell of decay'.[5] Image is thus desocialized to become part of a cycle of life and death of which both the living members of village society and their deceased predecessors are stages distinguished in terms of 'smell' and 'visibility' as the features characteristic of human life processes in general.

Because by the expulsion of his image the deceased has become 'incomplete', he strives for recompletion by reforging the connection between his body and someone else's image. He 'searches for an "image" among his kin to take with him', and if he succeeds it leads to another death. To prevent this, coins used to be placed on the deceased's eyes, breast, and hands, reconstituting an image out of money. By modifying the deceased's image as this was observed by the living it was considered possible to ensure that 'the deceased no longer saw the living'. The deceased as a consciously observing subject was replaced by the deceased as a body and an image made of money. These coins, which by their burial were withdrawn from circulation through social relationships, served as a substitute for the further withdrawal of human images from the society of the living.[6] Although the immediate transfer of the deceased's image from society to the domains beyond and the alteration of his bodily image with coins served to prevent another death among his kin, the living beings that belonged to his house were nevertheless affected by his death. The eyes of his 'elder and younger brothers' were likely to 'become blurred', reducing their ability to kill fish and game. Since these products were also sold for cash in regional markets, the influx of money into the society steadily diminished as well as a result of this increasing inability to 'see'.

The plants and the trees planted by the deceased – some of which also produce cash crops – no longer bear fruit either. Therefore, to this day, people may cut them down as soon as death has struck a house, whereupon people who do not belong to the house come to claim them as their property. In this way it is contrived that the cultivated plants come to 'belong' to the images of 'strange' houses, which enables them to bear fruit and reproduce again. Even the house built by the deceased may be destroyed. Ancestral property, however, is not to be touched (cf. Hueting 1922: 143).

The expulsion of the deceased's image from society affects above all his unmarried close female relatives. Among the Tobelo 'the impurity of the dead . . . sticks to the female descendants' (Hueting 1922: 145). (This explicitly does not mean the deceased's wife or his daughters-in-law.) Thus it has been reported that among the Tobelo of the Dodinga and Kau districts 'sisters and other close female relatives sat still and separate' at the funerary ritual and were served food by the daughters-in-law from plates which belonged to the deceased's house but which the latter took home afterwards – taking so many 'that nothing remains for the lord of the house' (Hueting 1922: 145). Among the Galela, an unmarried sister (or daughter) of the deceased was appointed to act as 'two-in-one' or 'twin' (Galela *sago*). Her hair was combed in a parting and she was addressed by her deceased brother's (or father's) name. At a man's death the brother-sister (or father-daughter) relationship was disrupted and incorporated by the sister (daughter) herself, and this disjunction between a woman and her brother's (or father's) image caused her own body to 'rot'. As 'two-in-one' she was not allowed into the village temple, where the ancestors would be 'repelled by her smell of decay'. From then on, she and the other marriageable women of the deceased's house were forbidden to marry; nor could marriage gifts be distributed in newly established affinal relationships.[7]

Pre-existing affinal relationships are modified as well. Among the Tobelo, on the death of a man his wife's relatives bring a gift of rice, plaited mats, and other items required for a proper burial. This gift serves to 'kill' the gift received by those relatives earlier during the deceased's marriage ritual. That gift had consisted of a set of weapons and a sum of money, the weapons evoking the ancestral images of the bridegroom's House and rendering the money 'alive'. At death, this 'living' part of the gift, transferred to the bride's kin without being alienated from the bridegroom's House, finally 'dies' as well.

One observes that the disjunction of a man's image from his body and its transfer to the domains beyond affects beings and things which depend for their 'being alive' on their relationship with that image. Cultivated plants and trees, unmarried women, and valuables 'die', begin to 'decay', or are buried. Affinal relationships are divested of their 'living' nature by the final alienation of particular gifts. The further influx of money and rice into village society and the existing circulation of rice and money among affinally related houses come to a standstill. This paralysis of circulation increasingly affects the relations between the living and their ancestors. As participants in this circulation system, the ancestors have to be regularly 'fed' with the image of rice, which is separated from the grains by ritual 'cooking' (*ho hakai*). Since this comes to a halt as well, the ancestors begin to 'feel hungry', and the danger that they will 'strike' (*ho tohua*) the living by 'consuming' their images instead – resulting in fatal illness – becomes more and more acute. There is also the danger of their withholding their protection from the living, exposing them to the attacks of those dead (*tokata*) whose images have never been reincorporated into society and who continue to seek image among the living. As in the course of time successive houses are struck by death, the village suffers from an increasing removal of image from society into the domains beyond. This affects all the relationships that constitute the houses, their people, their cultivated plants and valuables, and – last but not least – their affinal relations with other houses. These relationships cannot be re-established unless circulation is once again set in motion. This used to be effectuated in the pre-Christian second mortuary ritual.

THE PRE-CHRISTIAN SECOND MORTUARY RITUAL

Whereas a man's death affected the relations connecting his image to the beings and things that 'belonged' to him and his affinal relations, in the second mortuary ritual a different level of relationship was at stake. Then each village society acted as 'one House' (*o tau moi*), opposing other villages in competitive, latently antagonistic relationships. Each House encompassed the trunks mutually relating as elder and younger brothers, their 'in-married women' (*mol*oka*), and their affines (*geri-doroa, momo-l*oka*), the latter often residing in other villages. As participants in this ritual, all acknowledged themselves to 'belong' to the originator of the House's territory, hence to the temple (*halu*; Galela *seri*) in which this original ancestral image was depicted in carvings. These various relationships were articulated in the transfers made during the successive phases of the ritual.

Before the ritual could be performed, the younger brothers and/or sons of the deceased had to amass large amounts of money. This was partly collected overseas, mostly by selling game, fish, and resin in the regional markets of Ternate and Tidore and partly by borrowing or claiming the restitution of loans from the elder and younger trunks of the House. Large amounts of rice had to be available as well, with the result that the ritual, ideally performed among the Tobelo once every five years, took place shortly afer each trunk had harvested its rice. The village temple, left to deteriorate since the ritual was last performed, was restored and decorated. Then the skeletal remains of the deceased were exhumed, cleansed of their perishable parts, wrapped in cloths and plaited mats, and put in newly constructed coffins. Each coffin was assigned a place inside the temple, presumably in accordance with the position held by the trunk of the deceased within the overall social order of village society.[8]

The first act[9] was the contribution of plates of uncooked rice by women married into each of the trunks to the trunks sponsoring the ritual. By the 'cooking' of this rice the image it contained was separated from it and offered to all of the ancestors of the House, from the founding ancestor (*wongemi*; Galela *wonge*) onwards (cf. Hueting 1922: 168–9). The same amount of rice but in cooked form, on the same plates, was then returned to the women. This transfer of the image of the rice to the ancestors of the House was required for the participation of the male trunk members in the ritual. Moreover, by contributing rice each trunk assured itself of the participation of the other trunks when they themselves organized the ritual in the future.

This opened the way for the unmarried girls of the village to begin noctural flirtations with boys from other villages. These flirtations, which took place as long as the ritual lasted, would eventually lead to the establishment of new affinal relationships with other Houses. Apparently the transfer of the rice's image to the ancestors released the marriageable girls, whose life was generated by these ancestral images, from the 'decay' in which they had participated since death had struck their House. On the next day, the male members of the House completed the restoration of the temple and constructed a vegetable token (*weka*) signifying that the deceased had died a heroic violent death. In the night that followed, in-married women performed dances in tribute to this token. The relationship between these women and the deceased's token was signified by the transfer to them by the sponsor of money 'belonging' to the deceased. This money, part of which had been acquired by the deceased with the assistance of his ancestral images, testified to his heroic deeds. This heroic image was distributed among the in-married village women.

The distribution of the monetarized image among the women at night provided them with the 'violent' character which they displayed the next day. Dressed as male warriors carrying the token of the heroic deceased and followed by their unmarried daughters, they paraded through the neighbouring villages, 'seizing' vegetables and fruit and passing these on to their daughters. Displaying the conjunction between themselves and the deceased's image – in its diurnal aspect of violent warrior – they collectively enacted the subordination of other villages to the House they had married into. On that day also the skeleton of the deceased was reconstructed from bamboo. As many pieces of barkcloth and parrot feathers were stuck into the ten 'joint cavities' as raids in which the deceased had participated. His 'twin' sister, still invested with his name, was made up with red fluids representing the 'blood' which he had shed during these raids. Bearing his weapons, she carried this skeleton frame around the temple. Whereas the image of the deceased was distributed among the in-married women in the fragmented form of money, providing them with the image of violent warriors, the image and the name of the deceased were attached to his unmarried sister or daughter in the form of his victims' blood, providing her with an equally violent image.[10]

In the next phases of the ritual, the relations between the village trunks and those trunks of the House whose members resided in other settlements were articulated. The in-married women of the latter trunks, who had contributed earlier to the initial rice offering, came in that night, dressed in expensive clothes and jewellery. It was understood that their husbands' trunks 'owed' these valuables to the heroic ancestors of the House. The women brought with them great quantities of rice and received large sums of money in return. These transfers – in opposite directions – of (un)cooked rice and money in the relationships constituting the House at its highest morphological level preceded the construction, the next day, of the 'emblem of the settlement' (*o berera ma ngale* 'the reason/cause of the settlement'). This emblem identified the founding ancestor of the House in relation to its territory of land and water. That day, male members of the elder and younger trunks living in other settlements consecutively paid tribute to this emblem in a war dance. Each time the same chest with money and valuables was placed at their feet by the sponsor of the ritual, and each time it was immediately taken back. The chest, evidently containing the inalienable heirlooms of the House as a whole, was not the object of a gift in the strict sense of the word. The act was an investiture with the House's indivisible heirlooms which signified the subordination of the males of the various trunks to the ancestral images of the House as a whole. When a dancer had offered his tribute and had been subjected to this investiture, he received a few coins. This token sum contrasted sharply with the large sums of money transferred earlier to the trunks' in-married women in return for the rice's image. One also observes the contrast between the circulation of rice and money at night and the non-circulation of the House's inalienable and indivisible heirlooms during the day. This nocturnal fragmentation of ances-

tral image among the in-married women and the diurnal unifi-
cation of trunks represented by male warriors were contrasting
parts of the same encompassing idea of the House.

That night a communal meal took place. Now the clothes and
the jewellery which the trunks 'owed' to the House's ancestors
and which had been displayed earlier by their in-married women
adorned their male members. Affines also took part in this meal.
Men who had married daughters of any of these various trunks
contributed palm wine, and, as their wives' 'fathers' and wives'
'brothers' had done during the day, they danced the war dance
in tribute to the founding ancestor's emblem. The House's heirlooms were placed at the feet of these collective 'daughters'
husbands' as well, and again they were immediately taken back
to be replaced by a few coins. The fact that the representatives
of trunks which had taken women from the House in marriage
were subjected to the same act of investiture as the elder and
younger brothers of the House indicates that in this phase of the
ritual the established affinal relationships were transformed into
relations between elder and younger brother trunks of one
House. While this was taking place, the nocturnal flirtations of
the marriageable girls of the House with potential bride-grooms,
which would eventually lead to a new generation of affinal
relationships, continued.

The following day, the in-married women and their marriageable daughters danced around the deceased's skeleton token and
the 'twin' sister around the founding ancestor's emblem. Each
woman received a sum of money. After this final distribution of
fragmented monetarized 'image' among the in-married women
and their daughters – the 'twin' sister being one of them – a
'meal of the grave' was served. This marked the fact that the
deceased's 'image was completely free of his body' and could be
incorporated among the ancestral images of the House. The
'twin' sister was divested of his name; from then on she no
longer encompassed the relationship between herself and her
brother. She received part of his estate in land and/or valuables.
The incorporation of his image into village society rendered her
unequivocally 'alive' again. A final parade was held in which the
unmarried daughters, instead of their mothers, were dressed as
warriors. Roaming through neighbouring villages, they simulated
the capture of unmarried boys and 'forced' them to stay to
partake in the last nocturnal flirtations. During the meal that

followed these boys were instructed, just as the bridegroom is exhorted during the marriage ritual, 'to eat very little', as if they were already a new generation of bridegrooms.

The incorporation of the deceased's images was effectuated by the transfers made in the second mortuary ritual. This not only entailed the articulation of all the relationships which made up village society but also brought about a shifting of the positions occupied by persons in this system of relationships. Sons succeeded their deceased fathers (younger brothers their deceased elder brothers); daughters assumed the marriageable positions once occupied by their mothers; 'strange' boys assumed the position of potential daughters' husbands; and, finally, daughters' husbands assumed the position of elder and younger brothers of the House. Rather than being a property of the kin terminology system as such (cf. Platenkamp 1988a: 61–75), this incorporation of affines into the House, entailing the transformation of affinal relationships into 'consanguineal' ones, could be effectuated only through ritual. This collective 'movement' of people through the system of relationships was accomplished by the setting in motion of the circulation paralysed by death. In other words, the system of relationships constituting village society as a whole was itself conceptualized as a system of circulation.

Rice and money figured prominently in this system. On the one hand, the indivisibility of the House was expressed in the investiture of the males of the House with its inalienable heirlooms of money and other valuables. On the other hand, each trunk transferred the image of the rice which it had grown on its own plots – withdrawn from the autochthonous owners of the land – to the founding ancestors of the House and received image in fragmented monetary form in return. This money had been collected abroad by the conversion of those marine and other animal species which embody not the image of one's own ancestors but the ancestral images of other, potentially hostile people and which are killed with the assistance of the ancestors (Platenkamp 1988a: 136–40). The circulation – entailing the conversion of the image of the rice into the image of money – thus followed upon the 'removal' of the autochthonous owners of the land from each cultivated plot, on the one hand, and the 'violent' subordination of 'strange' ancestral owners of people and animals, on the other. Once this circulation had been set in motion, 'strange' houses could be 'subordinated' to village society by its 'warrior' women and assigned the position of potential affines. This made possible the transition from the higher morphological level on which 'strange' Houses related to one another as potential enemies to the lower level on which trunks belonging to these 'strange' Houses established affinal relationships with one another.

THE MARRIAGE RITUAL

In contrast to its effect on the second mortuary ritual, Christianity has not fundamentally changed the ritual in which affinal relationships are established in Tobelo. The acts constituting this ritual, documented in detail elsewhere (Platenkamp 1988a: 190–224; Nijland 1985), can be divided into three series. First, there is the presentation, at night, of sago, palm wine, and fish and/or meat by the bridegroom and his kin (people on the man's side) to the bride's kin (people on the woman's side); afterwards a communal meal is served at the bride's home. This is followed some time later and in the daytime by the 'covering' (*ha tatoko*) of gifts contributed by the woman's side with gifts contributed by the man's side. Finally there is the transfer, also during the day, of the bride to the bridegroom's House, followed by a communal meal there.

The second series of acts, that of 'covering', is considered the core activity, establishing the affinal relationship as 'true'. This series takes place in the absence of the bride and bridegroom in a lean-to which his male relatives have attached to her house. In this phase of the ritual, the affinal relationship is projected in space as if the bridegroom's kin were being incorporated into the bride's house, a house that is part of the village which had collectively 'captured' its potential bridegrooms at the end of the second mortuary ritual. Inside the lean-to, a canoe-shaped table is constructed (the canoe being a model of affinal relationships) on which female relatives of the bride display cone-shaped baskets filled with uncooked rice, rice cakes, and plaited mats. Female relatives of the bridegroom then bring in a set of weapons and plates filled with money. The set of weapons, called 'the replacer of the site/container' (*o ngi ma dagali*), consists of a shield, a spear, and a sword tied together with a white headcloth. The plates of money are called *huba*. Once the weapons, the money, and other food gifts have 'covered' the rice and plaited mats, the items are taken up by women from each receiving party. The weapons are accepted by a male elder representing the bride's House as a whole.

The relationship between the weapons and the money is of great interest. The weapons are designated as 'the owner of the *huba*/the true *huba*' (*o ngi ma dagali o huba ma dutu*). The shield in particular bears witness to the heroic ancestral images of the bridegroom's House. It is construed as a person: in addition to 'arteries', 'spine', 'head', and 'feet', the shield has 'eyes' made of pieces of porcelain or mother-of-pearl that refer to the number of people killed by the ancestors of the bridegroom's House. In this context the weapons themselves are not 'alive', but in conjunction with the money they render the *huba* 'alive' (*o tiwi ma ngango* 'living money'). In other words, the relationship between the weapons as an objectified ancestral image and the money is conceptualized as part of the overall life-giving relationship between the ancestral images and the bodies of the people, plants, animals, and valuables which belong to these images.

This life-giving conjunction between the money and the ancestral images of its giver – represented in the weapons – is not severed upon their transfer, for under certain conditions the living money 'comes up floating'. When a marriage is dissolved because of the bride's misconduct, the living money must be returned to its giver, and in the event that the bride has borne children the sum restored should be twice the amount originally transferred. Living money, therefore, 'grows', that is, its value multiplies in accordance with the multiplication of the bride's children. This 'living' quality of the money remains dependent upon its relationship with the bridegroom's ancestral images, as represented by the weapons received by the bride's relatives. Hence, if upon divorce the money is not returned, then the weapons 'come alive' to 'eat', that is, to kill, the bride.

This composite gift of weapons and money, considered a 'living being', will 'take the place' of the bride in her parental house. However, before this 'replacement' can occur, the weapons and the money must first 'cover' the large quantities of rice and the sleeping mats during the second series of ritual acts. Not only is it inconceivable for the bride's relatives to omit to present the rice and the mats – their title to the money and the weapons is dependent upon their ability to provide them – but these transfers are prerequisites for the transfer of the bride to the

bridegroom's House. This indicates that the transfer of the bride
is itself part of and subordinated to a wider process in which
weapons and money – conceived of as living beings – on the one
side and rice and plaited mats on the other circulate in opposite
directions. It is for this reason that the visual representation of
this relationship, composed of weapons and money versus rice
and mats conjoined on a canoe-shaped table, is embued with
value for the Tobelo: it forms the core symbol[11] of affinity itself
(cf. Nijland 1989: 198–9). After these transfers have been made,
additional rice-money exchanges conclude this second series of
acts. Women from the bride's house offer plates of rice cakes to
members of the bridegroom's House, and the latter later return
the same plates filled with money. It is stressed that the rice
should not be valorized as a market commodity: the money given
in return must amply exceed the price paid for uncooked rice in
the local shops.

Only after these transfers have been accomplished do the
weapons and the living money 'take the place' of the bride in
her parental house, and only then can the bride be brought to
the bridegroom's. This transfer seems to involve her being severed from the ancestral images of her own House. Such a severance would be lethal (witness such statements as 'the bride leaving for the bridegroom's house departs to her grave') were it not
that prior to her actual transfer another image-body relationship
is constructed, and, again, money plays a key role. Women from
the bridegroom's House enter the house of the bride to decorate
her face with white dots and her breasts with coins. These coins
are part of the inalienable heirlooms of the House to which the
bridegroom's trunk belongs. In this way a conjunction is forged
between the bride's body and the money (testimony to the ancestral image of the bridegroom's House), a conjunction which in
itself is life-giving. At that moment the bride represents the
transcendent relationship between body and ancestral image. To
this representation the bride as a subject is subordinated: she
must not see this composite image, an image which literally is
not her own, reflected in a mirror, and therefore the mirrors in
the bedroom where she is being dressed and adorned are covered
(Nijland 1989: 209–10).[12] She is then escorted by women married
into the bridegroom's House to the latter's village. From then on,
she 'belongs' to the ancestral images of her husband's House.[13]

CHURCH AUCTIONS AND NEW YEAR'S PARADES

The transfers made in the pre-Christian first mortuary, second mortuary, and marriage rituals are stages of an overall system of circulation that involves village society and various domains beyond, among them that of image-less beings and those of the unspecified 'other people' with whom each village society stands in antagonistic opposition. These transfers of beings and things between the village and the domains beyond ensure the continuity and renewal of the relationships which constitute village society. Two interconnected cycles and two morphological levels of circulation can be discerned. At one level, the continuity of the trunks entails the reproductive multiplication of both people and crops. At this level the separate trunks and their male/female intertrunk relationships, modelled on processes of vegetable reproduction, are at issue. These relationships are conclusively established in marriage rituals by the transfer in opposite directions between trunks of living beings (bridegrooms, brides) and of things (weapons and money, rice and mats) valorized as living beings. These relationships are terminated at death, when the transfer of the deceased's image from the village to the domains beyond results not only in the death and decay of his body but also in the death of those beings and things whose life was generated by their conjunction with that image. The continuity of this cycle of life and death demands a shift to another level of circulation which involves the transfer of beings and things from one cycle to another.

In pre-Christian times, this was effectuated in the second mortuary ritual. Before money, rice, and brides could be transferred in affinal relationships and be placed in the conjunction with the ancestral image which allowed them to 'grow' and multiply, they had to circulate in the higher-level relationships which connected the elder and younger trunks to the founding ancestor of village society as a whole (cf. Parry and Bloch 1989 tracing similar contrasts). It is in terms of this configuration of ideas and values that the Tobelo and the Galela are eminently comparable to other eastern Indonesian societies (Barraud and Platenkamp 1990). Thus the image of the rice harvested from each trunk's garden plot was transferred by its in-married women to the village ancestors, while the money earned by the conversion of beings 'killed' abroad was transferred in the opposite direction.

These noctural movements, which articulated the unified and – at the same time – differentiated morphological structure of the House, alternated with diurnal acts performed by males and females alike under the aegis of the founding ancestor. The males paid a warrior's tribute to the founding ancestor and received an investiture with his inalienable heirlooms; the females – adopting a similar warrior role – mimicked the violent subordination of enemy villages, thereby initiating the transition from the higher-level antagonistic relations between enemy Houses to the lower-level affinal relations between them (hence perhaps the ambivalence of these females' role).

This pre-Christian conceptualization of society, operative in rituals some of which were observed almost a century ago, places the present-day church auctions and New Year's parades in a particular perspective. The fact that the rice and the money which the Tobelo still transfer in affinal relationships are also transferred in church, first by the members of the village community and then by those of different villages, indicates that the higher level of morphology nowadays is articulated in terms of church membership. At this level society consists of the relationships connecting the trunks that make up a village – in relation to other villages – with the Christian God. It is in these relations that the rice and money brought in from beyond apparently should circulate before they can be transferred in affinal relations. This also establishes the connection between these church transfers, made after the rice harvest, and the parades performed at the New Year. I suggest that, on the latter occasion, the village women still collectively mimic the subordination of enemy villages, thereby initiating the transition from the higher level to the lower level of affinity.

That these parades are no longer performed on the same occasion as the church auctions may be connected with the fact that the cosmological cycle, as measured in annual periods, no longer coincides with the agricultural cycle. In former times, both cycles were governed by the cycle of the Pleiades, but since the introduction of an agricultural reform and of the Gregorian calendar they have become disconnected (Platenkamp 1988a: 36–43). However, the New Year's parades still follow upon a collective commemoration of the village dead whose images have been definitely dissociated from their bodies – only those dead receive tombstones on their graves – and this reference to the images of the dead still provides the women with a warrior image. And, finally, the circulations of rice and money in church still precede these parades, just as they did during the pre-Christian second mortuary ritual.

This analysis of the church auctions is supported by several observations. The first concerns the notion of the founding ancestor of village society, the ancestral source of its image. According to the pre-Christian ideology, ancestral image manifested itself not only in the productive multiplication of people and plants but also in the capacity of males to subordinate 'strange' people and animals by violence, withdrawing image from them and having this image (in the form of money, valuables, and names[14]) circulate in the relations that constitute village society. Economic practice has changed, however. The money that enters the village nowadays is earned by the sale of cash crops, particularly copra, and as far as I know, in such agricultural activities no reference is made to the violent ancestral images.

This ancestral ability to subordinate 'strange' people by violence is under attack in other contexts as well. To give but a few examples, personal names are no longer violently sundered from 'strange' animals but selected from the Bible, albeit preferably from the Old Testament. The 'medicines' embodying the ancestral image that turns the warrior's mind 'hot' should, according to some, be replaced by bibles and psalm books. Thus a Tobelo soldier of the regular Indonesian army to be engaged in military action was provided by his father with a bible instead of the ancestral war medicines. However, his ancestors visited him in a dream, told him that his father was a coward, and provided him with the 'medicines' after all. Other Tobelo soldiers testified that on this occasion their ancestral images had 'preceded them to the battlefield'. Some people advocate that the set of weapons which in the marriage ritual is transferred to the bride's relatives also be replaced by a bible. It appears, then, that the Bible tends to become a transformed representation of the ancestral source of image. This transformation does not go unchallenged. It is said that the ancestors themselves, no longer being actually 'fed', take what is due to them by consuming the images of their progeny, with the result that 'since we have become religious our children fall ill more often'. It is in countering such statements that the Protestant ministers confront the holistic nature of Tobelo society with the individualistic tenets of Protestant Christianity; it is repeatedly preached from the pulpit that ancestors do not punish the living, that one is not responsible for 'feeding' their images (which 'are mere devils' anyway), and that each person will be judged for his acts only by God.

However, the very fact that the money, along with rice and mats, still circulates at the higher morphological level indicates that the lower level of affinity still derives its value from its relation to this higher level on which village society is conceived as part of an encompassing socio-religious whole. This suggests that the Christian church itself is valorized in reference to this holistic conceptualization of society.

NOTES

1 This analysis is based on fieldwork conducted mainly in the southern part of Tobelo district for some twenty months in 1979, 1980, and 1982 and on archival research on Tobelo and the linguistically closely related neighbouring Galela, whose rituals have been well documented. Detailed descriptions of these rituals are in Platenkamp (1988a, 1988b, 1990); extensive source references on pre-Christian rituals are in Platenkamp (1988a). Field data on the New Year's parades performed nowadays in the Tobelo village of Paca were generously put at my disposal by D. Nijland and A. Nijland-Bleeker. Financial support was provided by the Netherlands Foundation for the Advancement of Research in the Tropics (WOTRO). The field researches were conducted under the auspices of the Lembaga Ekonomi dan Kemasyarakatan Nasional (Jakarta). I am indebted to the members of the Cognitive Anthropology – Structural Anthropology research team (ASA) of Leiden University and of the Equipe de Recherche d'Anthropologie Sociale: Morphologie, Echanges (E.R.A.S.M.E.) of the Centre National de la Recherche Scientifique, Paris, for their valuable comments on a previous version of this article and to R. Robson for her careful correction of the English text.

2 This act identifies the mythical emissary as the prototypical shamanistic healer. In healing rituals, a shaman's familiar spirit may travel to the lord owner to 'purchase' a 'depiction' (*tulada*) which is subsequently 'inserted' as image into a patient's body. The latter then once again displays 'living' movement.

3 Although the first and second mortuary rituals are no longer performed in their pre-Christian form, this and other ideas discussed presently are still maintained by the Tobelo. To describe these I therefore use the present tense, reserving the past tense for the discussion of ideas and acts which definitely are no longer part of this society.

4 They are said to recognize living people by the smell of their bodies, and any object withdrawn from these owners of the land must be marked with urine, blood, or saliva. Shamans who can 'see' them emphasize that their faces cannot be identified; nor do they have personal names. The *moroka* in particular lead a parallel existence in invisible settlements in the forest where the soil has not yet been exploited for agriculture. Before a plot is cleared and rice is sown, their removal is induced by bringing small offerings.

5 The transfer of the deceased's image is compared to the movement of a person from one settlement to another. Having arrived at a 'strange' place, one 'must be placed under the protection of the "owner" of that place so as to avoid wandering about lost'.

6 The living could also trick the deceased into believing that they were image-less beings themselves. To this end they would blacken their faces with mud, soot, or ashes, pretending that they themselves were decaying bodies from which no image could be taken.

7 If a marriage was nevertheless proposed, a large sum of money in addition to the usual sum would have to be transferred to the bride's house to replace the deceased's image, a replacement that would ordinarily take place in the second mortuary ritual. By the transfer of the money a new relationship was forged between the brother's image – represented by money – and the sister, terminating the 'decay' of her body and rendering her 'alive' again.

8 See Visser (1989) for an analysis of the way in which, during a very similar ritual performed by the related people of Sahu, the social order is spatially expressed in the positions assigned to the participants in the village temple.

9 A comparison of the scant data on the Tobelo ritual with the detailed data recorded among the neighbouring Galela reveals a high degree of similarity between their second mortuary rituals. The available Tobelo data are understandable when interpreted as part of a structure that also orders the Galela data (Platenkamp 1988a: 164–89). (On this procedure, involving a structural comparison of societies within a 'field of anthropological study', see Josselin de Jong [1980].) The following summary is largely based on these Galela data.

10 This procedure parallels that of the former male initiation ritual, whereby violent ancestral images were inserted into the initiates in the form of fluids representing 'blood'. This made their 'awareness' (*hininga*) 'hot' and rendered them capable of participating in raids (Platenkamp 1988a: 144–8).

11 '*Symbolon* . . . meant precisely a piece of something that was the token of the remaining part and that had to be completed by it to be recognized as a *symbolon*. Each was the token of the other' (Valeri 1980: 191).

12 Using a film registration of the ritual as a stimulus to a Tobelo audience, Nijland (1989: 209–10) elicited important information concerning this idea. Not only should the bride – as well as her female relatives – avoid seeing herself adorned with the ancestral coins, but

she and the bridegroom should also avoid seeing pictures of this even as long as twenty years afterwards.

13 She becomes subject to certain protective prohibitions which focus on the connection between her body and the water owned by the founding ancestor of her husband's House. For instance, people who do not belong to that House may not come into contact with water that has touched her body or her clothes. Heavy fines sanction this rule.

14 For example, in pre-Christian days an infant's image was 'strengthened' by the image embodied in a 'strange' animal killed by the father, consumed by the mother, and passed on through breast milk to the infant. The infant was then named after the animal.

REFERENCES

Barraud, C., and Platenkamp, J. D. M. (1990) 'Rituals and the comparison of societies', in C. Barraud and J. D. M. Platenkamp (eds) *Rituals and Socio-cosmic Order in Eastern Indonesian Societies*, pt. 2, *Maluku*, Bijdragen tot de Taal-, Land- en Volkenkunde 146, 1.

Barraud, C., Coppet, D. de, Iteanu, A., and Jamous, R. (1984) 'Des relations et des morts: quatre sociétés vues sous l'angle des échanges', in J-C. Galey (ed.) *Différences, valeurs, hiérarchie: Textes offerts à Louis Dumont*, Paris: Editions de l'Ecole des Hautes Etudes en Sciences Sociales.

Dumont, L. (1977) *Homo aequalis I : Genèse et épanouissement de l'idéologie économique*, Paris: Gallimard.

Hueting, A. (1922) 'De Tobeloreezen in hun denken en doen, 2', *Bijdragen tot de Taal-, Land- en Volkenkunde van Nederlandsch Indië* 78: 137–342.

Josselin de Jong, P. E. de (1980) 'The concept of the field of ethnological study', in J. J. Fox (ed.) *The Flow of Life: Essays on Eastern Indonesia*, Cambridge: Harvard University Press.

Nijland, D. J. (1985) *Tobelo Marriage* (film), Leiden: Institute of Cultural and Social Studies, Leiden University.

——(1989) 'Schaduwen en werkelijkheid', Ph.D. thesis, Leiden University.

Parry, J., and Bloch, M. (1989) 'Introduction: money and the morality of exchange', in J. Parry and M. Bloch (eds) *Money and the Morality of Exchange*, Cambridge: Cambridge University Press.

Platenkamp, J. D. M. (1988a) 'Tobelo: ideas and values of a North Moluccan society', Ph.D. thesis, Leiden University.

——(1988b) 'Myths of life and image in northern Halmahera', in H. J. M. Claessen and D. S. Moyer (eds) *Time Past, Time Present, Time Future: Essays in Honour of P. E. de Josselin de Jong*, Dordrecht: Foris Publications.

——(1990) 'The severance of the origin: a ritual of the Tobelo of North Halmahera', in C. Barraud and J. D. M. Platenkamp (eds) *Rituals and*

Socio-cosmic Order in Eastern Indonesian Societies, pt. 2, *Maluku*, Bijdragen tot de Taal-, Land- en Volkenkunde 146, 1.

Valeri, V. (1980) 'Notes on the meaning of marriage prestations among the Huaulu of Seram', in J. J. Fox (ed.) *The Flow of Life: Essays on Eastern Indonesia*, Cambridge: Harvard University Press.

Visser, L. E. (1989) *My Rice Field Is My Child: Social and Territorial Aspects of Swidden Cultivation in Sahu, Eastern Indonesia*, Dordrecht: Foris Publications.

Chapter 6

Ritual implicates 'Others': rereading Durkheim in a plural society

Gerd Baumann

On the day when I began to draft this chapter,[1] a West London weekly newspaper local to my place of second fieldwork carried on its front page a large, imposing photograph. It showed a file of elderly men recognizable as Punjabi Sikhs by their bearded features and turbans and as veteran combatants from the arrays of medals pinned to their chests. Under the bold heading 'World War Heroes', readers were informed that 'Ex-Indian Army servicemen from Southall and Hounslow climbed a remote hill in Sussex for the annual service of remembrance at Britain's isolated and impressive Chattri Memorial'. The paper is delivered free to some 45,000 households in West London, at least a third of which are headed by persons of English extraction and another third by persons of Punjabi extraction. To native English readers, the photograph shows conspicuously 'foreign' men in the pursuit of a ritual that, instead of stressing their foreignness, establishes their claim to being 'of us': 'Thousands of Indian soldiers', the caption explains, 'fought and died in the trenches of World War One' (*Greenford, Northolt and Southall Recorder*, 29 June 1990: 1). London Punjabi readers, conversely, can see in the newspaper coverage of the ritual how a group of 'us', often forgotten or ignored, contributed to 'their' war victory, thus placing it in a shared history 'of ours'. News and photographs of such South Asian veterans' reunions appear several times a year in West London newspapers and in the national press aimed at South Asians in Britain.

The example may well evoke a reading inspired by the famous cover photograph of *Paris Match* that sparked Roland Barthes's semiological analysis of post-war French 'mythologies' (1973

[1957]). There, the photo cover of an African soldier in French uniform saluting the Tricolore signified, for Barthes, a mythological vindication of the values of empire and of multi-ethnic unity under its flag. There are echoes of this interpretation in the present example, yet it concerns not merely a posed photograph but a living ritual. Exemplary for my argument is the fact that a ritual has been used here to convey a message across a cultural cleavage to 'others' or to an outside 'public' and that this message is concerned quite centrally with reformulating the cleavage between 'us' and 'them'.

PURPOSE AND PROPOSITIONS

The following discussion addresses some further ethnographic observations of ritual being directed at an outside public or making statements about the definition or redefinition of outsider and insider in the ritual process. It thereby questions three assumptions that underlie much of our anthropological discourse about ritual. All three claim to derive from the axiom, privileged since Durkheim, that ritual is best understood as an act internal to the category or group that celebrates it or celebrates itself through it.

We tend to take it as given, on the whole, that rituals are symbolic performances which unite the members of a category of people in a shared pursuit that speaks of, and to, their basic values or that creates or confirms a world of meanings shared by all of them alike. The congregation, or ritual community, is assumed to share a relationship to the performance, its symbols, and their meanings and to be essentially concerned with itself. As Leach put it with genial clarity, in ritual, in contrast to a music recital, 'the performers and the listeners are the same people. We engage in rituals in order to transmit collective messages to ourselves' (1976: 45). The assertion, fundamental as it is to much of our understanding of ritual, fails to ring true in the sight of the newspaper photograph and in the sight of much ritual activity in plural societies and, as I shall suggest later, non-plural or 'ethnic' societies, too. The three assumptions ostensibly derived from it seem to me to reflect a narrow and one-sided reading of Durkheim rather than Durkheim's position itself.

Three propositions seem to me to arise from the data. First, instead of assuming that rituals are performed by congregations or ritual communities, I suggest that they may also be performed by competing constituencies. Secondly, instead of assuming that rituals celebrate the perpetuation of social values and self-knowledge, I suggest that they may equally speak to aspirations towards cultural change. Thirdly, instead of assuming that participation in ritual is limited to insiders, I suggest that we recognize the frequency of outsider participation not only in plural but also in non-plural societies.

In order to argue these three propositions, I will focus throughout on the capacity of rituals to implicate 'Others'. This capacity is shown in three different contexts. First, an examination of public rituals in a plural society shows how rituals can be 'addressed' to 'Others'. Such an address may be directed at non-participants or it may aim at co-participants of different constituencies within the same ritual. Secondly, an examination of two domestic rituals shows how 'Others' may be implicated not only as physically present addressees but, even in their absence, as categorical referents. In such cases, ritual can serve to negotiate the differing relationships of its participants with these 'Others' and in the process reformulate cultural values and self-knowledge. Thirdly, a brief examination of evidence from non-plural societies will suggest that outsider participation in ritual is widespread and that it is possible and useful to distinguish different modes of participation in any ritual.

My data were gathered in four years of field research[2] in a multi-ethnic suburb of London, Southall, which is a densely populated and comparatively discrete 'town' of some 66,000. The population of Southall is predominantly of Punjabi origin, with Sikhs from the Indian part of the region the largest single category, complemented by sizeable Muslim and Hindu contingents from either side of the Indo-Pakistani border. Their settlement in the area began in the 1950s and peaked in the early 1970s, with a separate influx of Punjabi families surrendering their family businesses and clerical posts to 'Africanization' in the East African countries. Alongside this internally heterogeneous Punjabi majority there are minorities of English, Irish, and Afro-Caribbean backgrounds, the latter drawn mainly from 'the small islands' such as Grenada, Dominica, St. Lucia, and Antigua. In a multicultural arena such as this, the presence of 'Others' and 'outsiders', however the context may define them, is almost a given when it comes to 'public' ritual.

PUBLIC RITUALS: THE PRESENCE OF 'OTHERS'

Whether or not these 'Others' are to be consciously addressed by a public ritual performance, their presence alone can suffice fundamentally to alter the intentions and meaning of a traditional ritual. Thus, an Anglican religious observance, the procession on Good Friday, takes on new meaning on the streets of a 'town' inhabited primarily by 'non-Christians': an Anglican Church in 1989 invited its congregation to a public procession expressly 'to witness the Death and Resurrection of Our Lord'. A traditionally inward-looking observance is here turned into one of outward-oriented 'witnessing'. Tellingly, some members of the congregation declined to take part lest their public observance be misconstrued as a reassertion of 'white', 'English' or 'Christian' claims to 'owning the streets'. Competitive relations enacted through ritual and addressed to outsiders are clearer in another case.

A Sikh temple, or *gurdwara*, favoured by families of the Jat caste and claiming a membership of 11,000 called for a procession to celebrate the founding of the Khalsa. This was in 1988, when such a procession had not taken place for seven years because of political conflict in the Punjab and related disagreements among several local Sikh congregations. In the event, the procession attracted some 20,000 participants (*Ealing Borough Guardian*, 28 April 1988: 1), among them local civic dignitaries and the Member of Parliament and several thousand Sikhs drawn from congregations other than the organizing temple. What had been demonstrated, in the words of the organizer, was 'the community uniting again' – uniting, that is, behind the leaders of the temple previously most at odds with the leaders and members of other Sikh congregations. The procession conveyed a symbolic message aimed quite specifically at these 'Others', the local public and Sikhs of other castes, other interests in the Punjab conflicts, and other political factions.

There are numerous cases of public ritual, religious, secular, or indeterminate, aimed as much at a symbolic statement to outsiders as at the consolidation of internal values and meanings. Public ritual in plural societies (and probably not only there) can very often be viewed as a claim to public attention, public space, and public recognition in an arena which allows and encourages multiple readings of symbolic messages. This is especially clear when the participants in a ritual do not even seem to form a ritual community but are recognized most easily as a loose alliance of ritual constituencies, each using symbolic forms to stake mutual claims. The official opening of a 'community sports centre' in September 1987 may help to clarify the issue.

The sports centre had been named, after much political wrangling, after an aged British peer intimately connected to the independence movements on the Indian sub-continent who regarded India as his 'spiritual home'. He attended the official opening as the guest of honour, accompanied by local politicians, administrators, and activists drawn from English, Punjabi, and Afro-Caribbean backgrounds and watched by an audience of local adults and youths. The ensuing ritual consisted of speeches by local politicans and the guest of honour (all Punjabi or English), the unveiling of a commemorative plaque, performances representing the local cultural heritages with a Punjabi dance troupe, and a sound system playing reggae music programmed by three Afro-Caribbean young men. The representation of musical cultures in this ritual was germane to a key problem facing public provisions in this multi-ethnic town: while Punjabi interest groups are well organized and influential in local politics, Afro-Caribbean youth and adults often express their at times angry dissatisfaction with the lack of youth and leisure provisions from which they suffer in West London.

Given this background, the official opening was, in many ways, a ritual enactment of conflicting claims regarding the new civic resource. The mayor openly acknowledged that 'some people might think that this centre is for Asian people only' but went on to stress that, in contrast, it was 'a centre for the whole community'. The guest of honour, on the other hand, addressed an audience some two-thirds of whom were white, as his 'fellow-Indians'. 'This speech sounded funny', commented an American eyewitness, 'coming on the heels of the mayor's assurance that the centre was not for Indians only'. Yet a representative of the borough proceeded to clarify, in a further speech, why the centre had been named after the peer. This allowed for a further set of claims, this time of a party-political nature, to be symbolized in the ritual. Already the mayor's speech had claimed the centre as a token of his administration's forthcoming 'Anti-Racism Year'. His official's explanation could now specify this claim: the decision on the centre's name was inspired by the peer's long association with the causes of anti-colonialism, the peace movement, and international socialism, all three the hallmarks of his own political party.

In summary, the civic ritual of the opening can be seen quite clearly to have followed one symbolic agenda at heart: the representation of claims, both to credit and to access, of one's own group as opposed to 'Others', however contextually defined. It may be argued now that such cases of ritual performance aimed at 'Others' are peculiar to public rather than private ritual. The distinction, of course, is highly questionable and vague at best, but even if it were clearer it would hardly suffice to cordon off ritual performed towards 'Others' from ritual as it 'should' be or ritual as one-sided readers of Durkheim would wish it to be.

FAMILY CHRISTMAS: THE 'OTHER' AS REFERENT

To develop the point, I shall cite data from two domestic rituals performed among London Punjabi families, Christmas and children's birthday celebrations. Both are, I contend, concerned quite centrally with defining and redefining relationships with 'Others'. Even when physically absent, these 'Others' are implicated as cultural referents, and the negotiation of relationships with them places ritual in the service of aspirations towards cultural change and new self-definitions.

The rituals of Christmas are, of course, hard to overlook and difficult to escape in any Western country. Commercial advertising and the mass media broadcast the triple messages of reciprocal presents, paid holidays, and family reunion for all, and the Christian religious symbolism has been augmented by a plethora of emblems which, like greeting cards and Christmas trees, Christmas pantos and office parties, have all removed the occasion beyond any useful distinction of sacred or profane, public or private. Sikh and Hindu families, too, have come, over the past ten to fifteen years, to celebrate their own Christmas rituals, albeit not, of course, in their religious symbolism. To illustrate the point, I adduce some extracts from the diary of a girl of sixteen which shows Christmas as an occasion of extended family gatherings among Sikhs of the Jat caste of farmers.

Saturday, Dec. 24th: Today, me and Mum went to my cousins' houses to give their Christmas presents. Then we came home and done all the housework. Apart from that it was a quiet day. The only good film on [television] was 'Jagged Edge'.

Christmas Day was great. All my relatives came round our house. We watched films on TV like 'Back to the Future' and 'The Empire Strikes Back'. I ate so many chocolates. We didn't cook a turkey because all my family are vegetarians, and most of my relatives. Instead we ate food like pakora and somosas.

More elaborate patterns of adoption and adaptation of the originally alien ritual are made clear in the diary of a fifteen-year-old girl of a Hindu family.[3] It is worth noting that preparations are initiated by adolescents on their own, to be followed only later by the involvement of parents.

Thursday, 8 December: While I was watching TV, the people kept on saying: 'Here are films for Christmas and programmes for your enjoyment.'

Friday, 9 December: It was the same as Thursday.

Saturday, 10 December: My sister and I started to gather our money together to buy Christmas presents. . . .

Sunday, 11 December: My sister and I talked about how much money we've spent so far on the presents. Then we talked about having a Christmas Dinner. We said we would have the following: turkey, Yorkshire Pudding, mince pies, gravy, apple-sauce, sprouts, ice-cream and jelly, nuts and a few other things. The turkey had to be stuffed.

Monday, 12 December: We got out our decorations and started to put them up. . . .

Tuesday, 13 December: The family were discussing to buy a Christmas Tree. . . .

Wednesday, 14 December: We went and bought a Christmas Tree. . . .

Thursday, 15 December: When the tree opened up its branches we decorated the tree. . . . with colourful round balls and tinsel. Everyone kept saying: 'Now we can put the presents under it'.

Friday, 16 December: I told my friends [at school] that I would give their presents on Monday [19 December] and started [to] give out my cards. People kept talking about Christmas holidays and how they were looking forward to a disco [at school] on Tuesday. . . .

Saturday, 17 December: We did nearly all our shopping and bought wrapping paper. You use that to wrap the presents. The wrapping paper is very pretty. . . .

Monday, 19 December: Today I gave my friends their presents. They all said thanks and seemed pleased.

Tuesday, 20 December: A day before our Christmas holidays we had a disco [at school]. A few people were carrying mistletoe. When I got home we put up our Christmas lights around the front room. It all looked very nice.

Wednesday, 21 December: At my last day of school of 1988, I gave my Christmas cards out, people gave me cards and said: 'Have a nice Christmas!' . . . I am very much looking forward to Christmas.

Thursday, 22 December: We bought the *Radio* and *TV Times* and started to mark what we was going to watch and record over the holidays. The TV kept showing things to do with Christmas and how to help the elderly people who spend Christmas alone. We decided not to have turkey but just snacks.

Friday, 23 December: Today I did all the last-minute shopping and all the food shopping. Wrapped any other presents which had been bought.

Christmas Eve, 24 December: Today I gave everybody their presents. The rest of the day I spent at [the] shop [where I work]. When I came home I just watched TV.

Christmas Day, 25 December: I was up bright and early. We all opened our presents, had chocolates, and pulled crackers. The rest of the day we just watched TV and ate.

Boxing Day, 26 December: Today I sat in front of the tele . . .

Wednesday, 28 December: Today I thought of saving up for next Christmas. Not much good stuff was on [television]. The tele keeps going on about Christmas programmes.

The extract shows clearly how the 'advent' of the Christmas 'season' is advertised by commercial media, how Anglo-American customs such as sending Christmas cards and holding Christmas parties are adopted among friends and peers, and how reciprocal exchanges of presents are taken beyond South Asian precedents. The examples of both girls also show, however, that limitations are imposed on the adoption of the Christmas ritual: replication stops short of indulgence in the traditional English

Christmas dinner, and even children who would like it are not enculturated into its exotic binary oppositions, which pair turkey with cranberry rather than apple sauce and Yorkshire pudding with beef rather than turkey. There are further limitations worth noting, and all of these are negotiated between children, often enthusiastic in embracing all the available symbols and emblems, and their parents and elders, more reluctant and selective in doing so. Thus, few parents engage in the customs and traditions connected to the figure of 'Father Christmas', who in the Christian tradition is based on Saint Nicolas and in the Anglo-American tradition is thought to deliver presents after descending through the chimney of the family home. London Punjabi Christmas presents are given and received face to face. Christmas carols, likewise, are extremely rare in London Punjabi celebrations, and I know of only one case among a Hindu family.

Both the replication and the limitation of Christmas rituals draw attention to the same critical relationship: it is triangular in that it involves parents vis-à-vis their children vis-à-vis the surrounding culture with its post-Christian traditions. The domestic rituals of Christmas seem to me a clear case of the performance of rituals which, in effect, negotiate the subtly differing relationships of youth and adults to surrounding 'Others'. For the children these 'Others' are their peers and school friends, with whom they discuss and compare their own family's celebrations. Alibhai (1987) mentions cases in which children exaggerate the extent of their family Christmas celebrations in order to protect their parents from being thought 'backward', traditionalist, or mean. The adults' visible 'Others', likewise, are fellow Punjabis, kin or neighbours, who again assess the merits of going too far or not far enough in replicating the originally alien ritual.

There are, moreover, what one might call the 'invisible Others', the category of 'the English' whom both adults and children know as a minority locally but as 'the' majority nationally. The Christmas ritual among London Punjabis can be seen, thus, as concerned essentially with 'Others' in that it negotiates, within each family, the relationship with these 'Others' and their customs and values. Such negotiation about the 'Other' enacted through ritual can assume surprising and subtle twists.

CHILDREN'S BIRTHDAYS: 'THEIR' RITES AND 'OURS'

Individual birthdays were not celebrated in the Punjab, and adults' birthdays are celebrated only rarely among Punjabi families in England. Children of Punjabi parentage, however, were aware of the birthday parties given for their English, Irish, and Afro-Caribbean peers, and their parents began to respond to this new expectation during the late 1970s. By the 1980s, most children of South Asian backgrounds had become accustomed to birthday celebrations; the completion of another year of life was thus recognized as an occasion worthy of celebration on autochthonous English precedents.

In the following, I give a brief account of a joint birthday celebration for two brothers of eleven and eight, eldest sons of a Punjabi-born Sikh couple of the Dhiman sub-caste who, now aged around forty, had come to Britain as adolescents in 1965.

The guests, all invited by the parents and grandparents of the two young celebrants, comprised six married couples, most of whose own children were being minded by other relatives at home. Two of the mothers had brought infants and toddlers and one had brought a child of perhaps five. These guests included the celebrants' father's elder sister and younger brother and their spouses and their father's mother's sister and her husband. These and the other guests were all classified as 'uncles' and 'aunts'.

All the women and children sat, chatted, cooked, and played in the combined kitchen-diner; all the men sat in the representative front room and were treated, from about seven in the evening, to Punjabi snacks, lager beer, and white rum. Conversation in the front room was desultory at best, and there was a definite lack of enthusiasm about the occasion relieved only by the celebrants' paternal grandmother, who came in to serve and was treated with the respect due a *ghar-da-wali* or 'mistress of the house' but did not sit down. The atmosphere was dull and purposeless in comparison with that of other social gatherings in which I had met some of the men, and also in comparison with the music, loud chatter, and good-natured turmoil in the women's and children's quarter. Towards nine o'clock, the celebrants' father invited all the men to proceed to the kitchen-diner and join in the celebration proper. Careful preparations had been made in setting up a large table with wrapped presents and the large shared birthday cake popular in many English homes and in borrowing a video camera and lighting equipment to record the celebration ritual.

The core ritual required all the adults and children to line up against the walls of the room while the celebrants and their mother stood behind the table laden with presents and the birthday cake, all in full view of the video camera. All by-standers sang the customary English 'Happy Birthday' song as the mother guided the older, then the younger son in cutting their cake. English custom would now require the celebrants' distributing their birthday cake to all well-wishers, but the ritual, at this stage, was inverted. Each adult stepped forward in turn and fed the older boy, then the younger boy a piece of the cake.

After the feeding ritual, the celebrants were guided by their mother and recorded on video by their father as they unwrapped their presents – toys, clothes, and books. Before they did so, however, the men were shown into the front room and served a Punjabi meal. Those who ate quickly and wished to, walked back into the kitchen-diner, where the birthday table had been moved out of the way, and women and children danced the *bhangra*, a Punjabi folk dance. Men were welcome to join in a spirit of light-hearted enjoyment; those who did, usually the younger ones, sometimes danced with the celebrants or with infants and toddlers in their arms. Towards eleven o'clock, the music was switched off and guests took their leave, hearty, respectful, or sullen, of their adult hosts.

Several facets of this birthday party throw light on ritual, and not only 'public' ritual, as concerned with the 'Other'. Like the Christmas celebrations, it defines the place of adults and children towards, and in, a culture with peculiar ideas about tracing time, acknowledging individuality, demonstrating parental affection, and a host of other concerns that go with the Western birthday party. Yet it negotiates this relationship with a subtlety available perhaps only to ritual, music, and other non-verbal perform-ances. The case shows a number of significant differences which, with Needham (1983), one might perhaps see as reversals. Whereas Anglo-European birthday parties typically assemble peers of the celebrants, this and many other London Punjabi rituals assemble their elders. Whereas Western practice cele-brates the occasion every year and for each child individually, the present case involves two brothers in a joint celebration, and many other families celebrate birthdays only for auspicious years and suspend celebrations during inauspicious ones as well as years of family mourning such as follow certain cases of death among kin in England or 'back home'. The most striking reversal without doubt is to replace the ritual of the celebrants' offering cake to their guests by a ritual of elders' feeding the celebrants. To appreciate its symbolism is not an imposing task: the significance of feeding is anchored in the Sikh as well as the Hindu tradition and accessible not only to London Punjabis. Yet its potency seems multiplied when it is introduced into the context of a seemingly 'Western' birthday party.

The negotiation with which this family ritual is concerned, that of one's placement with regard to 'Others', seems so far to tend towards a reaffirmation of Punjabi rather than Anglo-European conceptions. Yet it would be wrong to overlook the departure from Punjabi traditions that the ritual also entailed. The performance of the *bhangra*, which may, at first sight, suggest traditional ways of celebration, is, in effect, anathema to these traditions. Until a decade ago, the *bhangra* was a dance performed by men at the harvest festival Bhaisakhi and accompanied by men's songs to a set of drums. The *bhangra* danced at the birthday party by women as well as men was of the genre known as *bhangra beat*, a British Punjabi creation of the 1980s which clothes traditional melodies in commercial disco-style recordings using drum-machines and electronic synthesizers. In their texts these songs draw on traditional Punjabi poetry no more often than on new and sometimes controversial texts (Baumann 1990). Further warning against a misleadingly 'traditionalist' understanding of the ritual is provided by the adult men attending it: it is hard to imagine London Punjabis attending a celebration in a less festive mood, with less capacity for enjoyment and less sense of purpose, than the medley of classificatory uncles assembled in the celebrants' parents' front room. This is not surprising, however. As the celebrants' father's younger brother (*thaia*), an accountant of thirty-one explained:

> In my time, we never had birthdays in the family. I never had one, and . . . no, I didn't have a coming-of-age either. It wasn't done in the Punjab, and we didn't do it here. But with the kids, it's different, isn't it? They love it, and they need it here: they know their friends have it, too . . . You see, it's like Christmas: you adjust to the new society, and you give

the kids what they need here. I mean, if you don't, you're an outcast, isn't it?

The parallel, entirely unsolicited, touches the core of my argument: that the rituals I have described (and probably not only these) are concerned with negotiating relationships with 'Others', however contextually defined. In 'public' ritual, the presence of 'Others' is virtually assured in plural societies; in the domestic rituals discussed, the 'Others' may be visible family, neighbours, and friends or 'invisible Others' to whom one's relationship needs to be defined and negotiated. In all cases, the Durkheimian vision that underlies much of our understanding of ritual appears less than complete and leaves out most of what makes an ethnographic observation of these rituals worthwhile.

To draw together the argument so far, I should like to recapitulate the three understandings that we tend to take for granted but that it may be useful to question. First, instead of assuming that rituals are performances of homogeneous congregations or communities, it may be useful to think of them as resources competed for and used by various 'constituencies'. Just as a constituency comprises a medley of divergent actors and interests converging on one of a limited number of options, so a ritual constituency comprises all those who, for divergent and even mutually exclusive reasons, happen to converge on a particular routinized performance. Christmas rituals, with their converging constituencies of Christians and non-Christians, consumers and marketing experts, adults and children, may provide a very obvious example. Some symbolic performances may indeed be classified as different rituals by different participants. Thus, the funeral procession of a London Punjabi murdered, in 1990, by a native Englishman was understood as a demonstration against racism by its organizers and some of its constituency while it was thought of as a non-political act of condolence and respect for the bereaved family by most others. In the event, members of the two constituencies faced each other in verbal argument, one chanting anti-racist slogans under banners of protest, the other trying to stop what they saw as 'this lack of respect'.

Further, rituals need not speak to values basic to the culture and self-knowledge of their performing constituencies. They can speak as clearly and centrally to aspirations towards cultural change and even assimilation, as they do in the case of London

Punjabi families adapting Western domestic rituals. Finally, instead of assuming the meanings and values of a ritual to be representative, in a circular way, of the congregation performing it, different modes of participation may be discerned among different participants. Public ritual, which often accommodates 'Others' as bystanders, spectators, invited guests, competing participants, validating witnesses, or even beneficiaries, presents many examples in point. All three propositions arose from the same attention to what in the purportedly Durkheimian understanding of ritual has little place: the implication of 'Others', be it as participants themselves or as the points of reference the relationship to whom needs defining and negotiating by the ritual constituency. Given the doubts cast on the three assumptions, the question arises whether evidence against them is limited to plural societies.

EVIDENCE FROM NON-PLURAL SOCIETIES

Just as most monographs envisage their 'ethnic' or 'tribal' societies as cultural wholes, so rituals tend to be portrayed as closed performances of unified congregations. The two may well be related. The closure in our conceptualization of society has been examined by Barth (1992); it may easily encourage closure also in our interpretations of ritual. In spite of such conventions, however, there is plentiful evidence that even in non-plural societies 'Others' are implicated in ritual and may indeed participate in socially differentiated ways. At least five distinct modes of participation appear from the literature. Where rituals concern only a sub-section of a society, there are, of course, likely to be (1) bystanders. While these are disinterested, (2) spectators participate as interested parties, whether in appreciation of the ritual performance or in depreciation of it. A more integrated mode of outsider participation is that of (3) the invited guest, asked along to lend a sense of occasion to the ritual or, as often, to enhance its recognition and status. The importance of spectators and guests is familiar to readers of Balinese ethnography from such works as Boon (1977) and Geertz (1980). Leroy (1979) describes spectators and guests of the ceremonial pig kill of the South Kewa as serving an even more integrated purpose: that of allowing elders to 'bring . . . irresponsible youths into line' with ritual demands they no longer fully endorse

(1979: 206). Ritual appears here not merely to thrive but to survive on the strength of outsider presence.

A first fully integrated degree of outsider participation is the mode one may call (4) 'witnessing'. Legal rituals such as oaths and many personal rites of passage may depend on the outside witness to confer on them not only recognition but validity. A further mode of participation of 'Others' may be recognized in that of (5) the outside beneficiary. Examples can be found in Nadel's ethnography of 'symbiotic ritual' among the Nuba hill communities of South Kordofan, where particular 'clans' are charged with performing rituals that are to benefit members of other local groups (1947: 9–10, 207–8). It is not a giant step from these differential modes of participation to the surmise that, in non-plural societies too, rituals may be conceptualized as having constituencies rather than unified congregations, as speaking to values of cultural change as well as continuity, and as implicating 'Others'.

From the same region as Nadel's, the Nuba Mountains of the Sudan, I should therefore cite some evidence collected during my first fieldwork between 1976 and 1979, which makes the three assumptions appear equally unwarranted in the setting of a society few would call plural. The Nuba of Miri, numbering some 3,000 sedentary agriculturalists of Black African descent, retain their own language beside the *lingua franca*, Arabic, and their own rituals of rain priests and possession priests alongside certain Islamic convictions and practices which have spread over the past five decades. Over the same period, the Miri have engaged in substantial labour migration to the country's urban centres, as have all their neighbours. The villagers' ritual calendars, none-theless, continue to be shaped by the seasonal celebrations of harvest festivals, centered on possession priests, and a rain-making festival, centered upon rain priests. This rain-making festival, Tanyara ma kola, is the high point of the Miri annual cycle and assembles several hundred villagers and as many migrants, as well as invited guests, in three days of dancing and ritual activity focused on the rain priests of a principal village. The central ritual on all three days is a dance of some 500 to 600 participants circling around the group of rain priests beating the ancient and sacred drum (*kola*) after which the festival is named.

While these rain priests and many villagers continue to profess the efficacy of the non-Islamic ritual in procuring rain, other villagers, most labour migrants, and all confirmed Muslims view it as a reunion of all Miri – villagers, migrants, and their offspring – to celebrate their unity across the rural-urban divide. In this regard, the ritual is directed at negotiating, among migrants and villagers, staunch Muslims and nominal ones, their relationships to an outside, namely, the surrounding society and culture of the metropolitan, Arabic-speaking, Muslim, urbanizing Sudan. The data, described in more detail elsewhere (Baumann 1987), are hardly exceptional in the context of African ethnography except perhaps for their emphasis on acknowledging from the start that all Miri profess Islam, that they follow their profession to different degrees, that at least a third live in cities rather than Miri villages, and that there are participants invited to observe rather than feel part of a unified ritual community. What I wish to stress here, in summarizing what appears as the epitome of the Durkheimian community celebrating itself, is the multiplicity of constituencies, ranging from the believers in ritual rain-making to committed Muslims, the multiplicity of values, ranging from a reaffirmation of rain priests' efficacy to a new affirmation of local unity despite recent cleavages, and the multiplicity of modes of participation, including spectators and invited guests.

Two provisos could be invoked, again to cordon off such a ritual from 'ritual as it ought to be seen' in the purportedly Durkheimian mould: the factor of Islamicization and the absence of 'Others' as defined on the 'ethnic' criteria we tend to use in plural societies. Yet both objections seem to fail in drawing a *cordon sanitaire* around Miri villagers' practice of 'traditional' ritual: for one, we know of very few African societies that have not experienced Islamicization, Christianization, secularization, or other religious change. Miri history is not exceptional in having divided a long-lost cultural uniformity into a plurality of values, religious convictions, and meanings recognized in traditional ritual. That such cultural uniformity and stability ever existed in any society is, in any case, not only a dubious but a highly ethnocentric assumption (Lévi-Strauss 1952).

As for the second reservation, that of an 'ethnic' uniformity maintained in non-plural societies but exceeded in plural ones, it, too, might beg the very question it purports to silence. How the 'Other' is defined is a matter of context alone; Hefner's (1985) work on the Hindu rituals of Tengger Javanese placed within a context of Muslim hegemony might be cited as evidence: even in an ethnically undifferentiated context, ritual may be as much concerned with a message to, or about, 'Others' as with what Leach called 'collective messages to ourselves' (1976:45). To attend to this possibility may well enhance our ethnographic understanding of the very distinction. The definition of 'us' and 'them' is not only contextual but intrinsically dialectical, and this dialectic can be a resource of ritual itself. In the ritual process, one mode of participation may be made to blend into another, ambiguities may be played out or manipulated, and constituencies may align and realign in the negotiation of who is 'us' and who 'them' through their modes of participation in the ritual process.

CONCLUSION

Narrow readings of Durkheim view rituals as crystallizations of basic values uniformly endorsed by communities that perform them with a view to themselves, ultimately to create and confirm their cohesion as communities. In plural societies, this position is complicated by the presence of 'Others', be it as 'visible' participants or as 'invisible' categorical referents. There it appears more useful to replace the idea of a ritual community with that of ritual constituencies, to widen the values celebrated from perpetuation to assimilation and cultural change, and to distinguish participation according to a variety of possible modes. All three propositions arise from the thesis that rituals, in plural societies, are concerned with 'them' as much as with the quasi-Durkheimian 'us'. Since 'us' and 'them' are always contextual and relative terms, it may be useful to trace the concern with 'Others' also in the ritual of 'non-plural' societies, once again questioning ethnographic accounts against the three propositions: to discern constituencies among seemingly homogeneous ritual communities, to recognize the reformative as well as the consolidating purposes of ritual, and to distinguish different modes of participating in the same ritual. This may allow us to do more ethnographic justice to the differing influences, interests, values, and modes of participation of different participants in any ritual.

These participants may include women alongside men, juniors alongside elders, recent participants alongside long-standing ones, converts alongside traditional adherents, guests alongside sponsors, clients alongside patrons, and one or more 'publics' alongside any 'community'. Ritual performances, symbols, and meanings may be directed at these as much as, if not sometimes more than, at the ritual core 'community' itself. There are 'Others' addressed through, or within, a ritual even when they all share the same ethnic denomination. Once we start looking out for these possibilities and for an awareness of them within ritual constituencies themselves, there is a good chance that we will find them also in seemingly non-plural societies. The classic Durkheimian vision of ritual as a society dancing, as it were, around the Golden Calf that represents itself may turn out to be a special case, to be located as such within a much wider universe of possibilities just as Euclidean geometry or Newtonian physics are special cases, if privileged ones, within systems of much wider currency and validity. If this is the case, monosemic interpretations of ritual can claim their rightful place as exceptions to the rule – provided that they can document that the readings of 'insiders' are all conclusive in unifying their symbolic referents regardless of 'Others'. This, however, would need to be documented rather than assumed. Durkheim's vision of the 'ultimate' ritual has always been knowingly essentialist.

Durkheim the ethnographer was fully aware of the participation of outsiders and of the implication of 'Others' in ritual: Discussing 'tribal unity' in the *Elementary Forms*, he insists that

> at the same time, it takes an international character. In fact, the members of the tribe to which the young initiates belong are not the only ones who assist at the ceremonies of initiation; representatives from the neighbouring tribes are specially summoned to these celebrations, which thus become sorts of international fairs, at once religious and laical . . . They invite to these feasts not only the tribes with whom a regular *connubium* is established, but also those with whom there are quarrels to be arranged.
>
> (Durkheim 1971: 294 and n.2)

Such data are cited by Durkheim only to help reconstruct the process by which Australian groups might have developed supratribal mythologies; they may be cited as usefully here to unearth Durkheim's theory from the rubble of assumptions heaped on it. 'What society is it that has thus made the basis of religion?' Durkheim asks of his own conclusion. 'Is it the real society, such as it is and acts before our very eyes . . . ?' (1971: 420). The answer is negative: 'society is not an empirical fact, definite and observable'; it is something 'in which [men] have never really lived. It is merely an idea . . . ' (1971: 420). Durkheim's theory applies to an abstracted essence of society, closer perhaps to what nowadays we call sociability or sociality and certainly far removed from 'society' in the empirical sense of an 'ethnic group'. To apply his great insight to any one empirical, externally bounded society is to fall victim to misplaced concreteness. The error exacts a high cost, since in order to maintain Durkheim's conclusions the ethnographer has to take for granted assumptions that Durkheim did not make and that the ethnographic record does not uphold. If these assumptions are 'Durkheimian', then Durkheim was not.

Durkheim's argument, essentialist and free of these assumptions as it was, enshrined, at a crucial time, the ideal case of all of a ritual's constituencies' confirming the same set of values from indistinguishable readings of the same symbols, thus conferring on their society, *qua* culture, the character of a monad. In a monadic society one might perhaps speak of 'the' meaning of any one ritual. 'Les monades n'ont point de fenêtres', postulates Leibniz in his *Monadologie*; but most existing societies do have windows, and define themselves, sometimes in ritual, by looking out of them.

NOTES

1 For the seminal idea for this chapter and a first thorough critique I thank Adam Kuper, who first suggested to me that 'in plural societies, people constantly watch each other's ritual; this should take its ethnography beyond the sharp distinction between ritual "insiders" and "outsiders"'. For helpful comments on a later draft of this chapter I thank Gunter Dabitz (Frankfurt) and Ralph Schroeder (Brunel University). The late Andrew Duff-Cooper (Tokyo) and Eric Hirsch (Brunel University) kindly alerted me to further ethnographic references.
2 My research was generously supported, in 1988–9, by a grant from the Leverhulme Trust, London; grateful acknowledgement is due to its chairman and board of trustees.
3 Warm thanks go to my friend and fellow researcher Marie Gillespie for her permission to use these diaries and for her unfailing support in the course of fieldwork and writing.

REFERENCES

Alibhai, Y. (1987) 'A White Christmas', *New Society*, 18 December, 15–17.

Barth, F. (1992) 'Towards greater naturalism in conceptualizing societies', in A. Kuper (ed.) *Conceptualizing Society*, London, Routledge.

Barthes, R. (1973 [1957]) *Mythologies*, trans. A. Lavers, St Albans: Paladin.

Baumann, G. (1987) *National Integration and Local Integrity: The Miri of the Nuba Mountains in the Sudan*, Oxford: Clarendon Press.

——(1990) 'The re-invention of *bhangra:* social and aesthetic shifts in a Punjabi music in Britain', in B. Wade (ed.) *Indian Musics*, The World of Music, special issue.

Boon, J. (1977) *The Anthropological Romance of Bali: 1597–1972*, Cambridge: Cambridge University Press.

Durkheim, E. (1971 [1915]) *The Elementary Forms of the Religious Life*, trans. J. W. Swain, London: George Allen and Unwin.

Ealing Borough Guardian (1988) 'Celebrations back after seven years', 28 April, 1.

Geertz, C. (1980) *Negara: The Theatre State in Nineteenth-Century Bali*, Princeton: Princeton University Press.

Greenford, Northolt and Southall Recorder (1990) 29 June, 1.

Hefner, R. (1985) *Hindu Javanese: Tengger Tradition and Islam*, Princeton: Princeton University Press.

Leach, E. (1976) *Culture and Communication: The Logic by which Symbols Are Connected*, Cambridge: Cambridge University Press.

Leibniz, G. W. (1890 [1714]) *Monadologie*, trans. C. J. Gerhardt, *Die philosophischen Schriften von G. W. Leibniz*, vol. 6, Berlin.

Leroy, J. (1979) 'The ceremonial pig kill of the South Kewa', *Oceania*, 49: 179–209.

Lévi-Strauss, C. (1952) *Race and History*, New York: UNESCO.

Nadel, S. (1947) *The Nuba: An Anthropological Study of the Hill Tribes in Kordofan*, London: Oxford University Press.

Needham, R. (1983) *Against the Tranquility of Axioms*, Berkeley: University of California Press.

Name index

Subject index